Frederick Pollock

**Personal Remembrances of Sir Frederick Pollock**

Second baronet, sometime queen's remembrancer. Vol. 2

Frederick Pollock

**Personal Remembrances of Sir Frederick Pollock**
*Second baronet, sometime queen's remembrancer. Vol. 2*

ISBN/EAN: 9783337324674

Printed in Europe, USA, Canada, Australia, Japan

Cover: Foto ©Thomas Meinert / pixelio.de

More available books at **www.hansebooks.com**

# PERSONAL REMEMBRANCES

OF

# SIR FREDERICK POLLOCK

SECOND BARONET

𝕾𝖔𝖒𝖊𝖙𝖎𝖒𝖊 𝕼𝖚𝖊𝖊𝖓'𝖘 𝕽𝖊𝖒𝖊𝖒𝖇𝖗𝖆𝖓𝖈𝖊𝖗

'Amicos habebat omnes bonos'
PHILELPHUS, *Vita Dantis*

IN TWO VOLUMES

VOL. II

𝕷𝖔𝖓𝖉𝖔𝖓
MACMILLAN AND CO.
AND NEW YORK
1887

# CONTENTS

## CHAPTER I

Queen opening Parliament—A Mormon meeting—Lord Derby's Administration—Decyphering—Goldsworthy Gurney—Ventilation of House of Commons—Duties of a Government—Babbage's workshops—Lord Melville—Lyme Regis—Funeral of Duke of Wellington—Publishers—E. V. B.—Ireland and the Jews—St. Mark's, Chelsea—Examining at Law Institution—Spiritual impostures—Applethwaite—Learning to read—Robson—The Wigans—Miss Horton—Tyndall—French play—Broadstairs—C. H. Townsend—Crystal Palace—Copley Fielding—Mr. Moore—Christ Church—Weymouth—Lyme Regis again . . . Page 1

## CHAPTER II

*Fortunio* at Tavistock House—Ossa on Pelion—Sir James Lacaita—A clever canvasser—Ffaringford—Dinner to Thackeray—Mr. Bellew—*Vie de Marianne*—Professor Thomson on heat—A cold spring—Tunbridge Wells—Sir Edwin's dogs—George Dyer—Bad French—Dinner in Albemarle Street—Babbage and burglars—A "Day-Peerage"—Naval review—Dinner at the Albion—Palmer's trial—Peace rejoicings—Illuminations—Ristori—*The Frozen Deep*—Crinolines—Cardinal Wiseman—Thackeray's lectures—Jacob Omnium—Professor Frankland—Chemistry of colours—Little Holland House—A christening party—Sir Richard Pollock—Changes in India—Emerson's *Orations*—Livingston—Definition of a fluid . . . . . . . . . 31

## CHAPTER III

The Comte de Paris—Buckle's lecture at the R. I.—Review of Buckle's history—British novelists—Toxophilite Society—Archers' Lodge—Ford—A. Froude—W. Spottiswoode—H. A. Merewether—Phelps as Sir Peter Teazle—*New Friends*—Russian scandal—Derby lotteries—Lord Blackburn—Vintners' Hall—Lord Wynford's speech—Smethurst's trial—Funeral of Macaulay—Sir Samuel Romilly—J. W. Parker—Books to read—*Fraser's Magazine*—Fechter's Hamlet—C. Kemble—Macready—Irving—Mounet Sully—Faure—Literary Fund dinner—Miniatures at Windsor Castle—Flint implements—Visits in Scotland—A Highland home—An elder of the Free Kirk—A mistaken minister—Lord Brougham at Brougham—Bonomi—Soane Museum—Death of Prince Consort . . . . . . . . . Page 68

## CHAPTER IV

A domestic play-bill—Lord Dundreary—*Antiquity of Man*—Dinner at R. M. Milnes'—Carlyle—Louis Blanc—Pitt and Bishop Tomline—C. Kingsley—Prince of Wales's wedding—A distressed damsel—"He has no children"—Max Müller—Jenny Lind—Geology at Freshwater—Napoleon III.—Archbishop Trench—Alfred Tylor—Phelps as Falstaff—Bishop Wilberforce preaching—Prince of Wales at Literary Fund dinner—Volunteer review—Bond's Horace—Dublin—*The Owl*—"Enoch Arden"—"Aylmer's Field"—Trial of Müller—Dinner to Berryer—A weekly journal—Writers in the *Reader*—Financial difficulties—Curiosities of editing—Mrs. Siddons—Tyndall's Ice Flower—A valentine—Lord Nugent and Campbell—A funeral sermon—Kate Terry—Some office work . . . . . . . . . . 103

## CHAPTER V

The Breakfast Club—First members—Access of offices and titles—*Ecce Homo*—Portraits at South Kensington—National Portrait Gallery—More on *Ecce Homo*—Reading of *Merchant of Venice*

## CONTENTS

— Sir Joseph Banks — *Twelfth Night* — Anthony Trollope —Writing by the calendar—Shakespeare and dogs—Sir Samuel Baker — Bournemouth — The new Latin primer — Governor Eyre—Want of courage in statesmen—Portland Prison—The November meteors—Dislike to gas—Chief Baron's collar—Mask of Shakespeare—Trinity Lodge—W. K. Clifford—Motley—Chief Justice Ellenborough—Death of Faraday—Switzerland—Fire in the Haymarket . . . . . . . Page 140

## CHAPTER VI

Montalembert — *Castle Rummelsberg* — A rejected voting paper—The Rolls Chapel—Statues in Burlington Gardens—Omission of Shakespeare—Representative figures—Leibnitz—Bacon—Goethe—Franklin—Priestley—Lord Normanby—Stage law—Disraeli at Literary Fund dinner—Sir Henry Holland—Merchant Taylors' Hall—Bishops and barons—City toasts—Fire in York Street—The Wigans—Wordsworth and Scott—Zurich—Peace congress—Fryston Hall—A brief dialogue—Mrs. Somerville—Privilege—Peel—Clerical merriment—Lord Kingsdown's *Reminiscences*—Campbell's *Life of Lyndhurst*—Sir George Cartier—Dickens as a reader—Political items—Cabinet Councils—*The Ring and the Book*—Error to the House of Lords—Lyndhurst and W. Holmes—Voltaire—Macaulay in Trinity College Chapel — Statue of Faraday — Frederick Locker . . . . . . . 170

## CHAPTER VII

Caen—St. Lo—Avranches—A watch lost and found—Mont St. Michel—A road adventure—French drivers—Hotel S. Romain—A case of identity—Tennyson at Haslemere—Bedgebury Park—Dilettanti Society—Avignon in Italy—Chloroform—Regnier—Brohan—W. K. Clifford—Franco-German War—Funeral at Hanworth—Clifford Harrison—French company in London—Plays at Opera Comique—*Dejener* at Crystal Palace—Speeches—Lord Dufferin—Lord Granville — William Spottiswoode — Clovelly — Westward Ho—Plays in Montagu Square—Mr. Evarts—A case of Latinity—Greenwich time—Disraeli—Henry Irving—Fitzgerald at Woodbridge—Miss Bateman's Medea—Portrait by Ouless—*The Ring and the Book*—Saunders and Ottley—Sir William Boxall . 209

## CHAPTER VIII

Theatre Français—Stage whispers—*Marion de l'Orme*—Lowell—Mohl
—Renan—Funeral of Macready—Desclée in *Frou-frou*—Fourth of
July—Fontainebleau—J. F. Millet—Rooms in the Chateau—
Madame Mohl—Paris under the Commune—Burning of Hotel
de Ville—Convention of Cintra—Retirement of Baron Martin—
Dinner at Garrick Club—Victor Hugo—Garrick and Shakespeare
—Wendell Holmes—Sir W. H. Walton—Queen's Remembrancer
—Duties of the office—City quit rents—Civic hospitalities—
Guildhall banquet—Trial of the Pyx—Goldsmiths' Hall—A Dowager . . . . . . . . . . **Page 247**

# CHAPTER I

### QUEEN OPENING PARLIAMENT

*28th January* 1852.—Babbage dined with us, and we went to the Marionette Theatre at the Adelaide Gallery. The piece was taken from the story of the *Bottle Imp*, and all was very cleverly managed. Babbage was delighted and very amusing, and was much interested in trying to find out how all the movements of the puppets were given to them. He was always good company when he threw off his grievances, and was with people whom he liked.

*3d February.*—Took J——, Fred, and Willie Richmond to see the Queen going to open Parliament, from the window of the room belonging to the Masters of the Court of Exchequer at Westminster. It was a cold day, and I put my wig on the little boy's head to keep him warm, in which he made a very comical figure, at which the Queen looked up and smiled.

*13th February.*—Laurence Oliphant dined, and to evening lecture at the Royal Institution. It was given by Grove, and he treated of electricity and magnetism, considered as states of matter rather than as distinct fluids. He showed some remarkable heating effects with a battery of 500 cells. Afterwards to Mrs. Barlow's.

*19th February.*—Dined Groves. Met Lyells, Brodies, Derwent Coleridges, Herman Merivales, Edward Romilly.

*22d February.*—With L. Oliphant to a Mormonite meeting at a music hall in Theobald's Road. As strangers we were put in a little gallery opposite to the platform. Many persons addressed the meeting, some with exhortations, and others with spiritual experiences and relations of miraculous cures—all extremely tedious and tiresome. Special notice was taken of our presence, and we were told of the time and of the place to which we could go to be taught more of their mysteries. Bread and wine, in celebration of the Lord's Supper, was handed round to each person coming in, on a tray like tea and cakes at an evening party. We came away impressed with the want of interest and the mean features of all that we had seen and heard.

*24th February.* — Long talk with Mr. Herries on the new Cabinet. It is not true that the Chancellorship of the Exchequer was offered to T. Baring. Palmerston is very cordial with them. Lord Derby had offered the Colonies to Mr. Herries, which he declined.

LONDON, 3*d March* 1852.

MY DEAR E.—A good deal has happened since I wrote last. The Whigs have rotted out of office, rather than been violently torn from it, and Lord Derby has formed a Government, which was despaired of by his friends last year. We are, of course, personally interested in the change, as it affects Mr. Herries. He was most anxious to avoid taking office at all, but has been forced to be where he is. In his position and with his name it would have been almost fatal to Lord Derby's plans if he had declined to be one of his Cabinet. The Board of Control keeps him out of the worry and fatigue of debate and interviews on matters of party politics, but it is an office of dignity, and just now of unusual importance, with reference to the question of the East India Company's charter. Other places of more prominence, but greater labour, were pressed upon him, but he chose to be what he is.—Yours affectionately, W. F. P.

*26th March.*—Babbage dined, and with us to Royal Institution. Cowper lectured on locks, with a description of the method pursued by Hobbs in picking Bramah's and Chubb's locks. This was a favourite subject with Babbage, and was akin to his love for decyphering, to which he gave much valuable time, and had a special dictionary prepared to assist in it, in which words were classed according to the number of letters in them, and arranged alphabetically, not only by the first, but by all the succeeding letters in them. I once invented a cypher and challenged Babbage to read it, but he declined to do so, on the ground that decypherers only accepted such challenges from persons of established reputation in the pursuit. I was not a foeman worthy of his steel.

*30th March.*—With Goldsworthy Gurney of Bude to evening sitting of the House of Commons, to assist him in observing the ventilation as conducted by Dr. Reid. His first introduction to London was effected by Lord Lyndhurst, and he was allowed to ventilate the

Court of Exchequer at Westminster, where I made his acquaintance and took much interest in his proceedings. He had been a successful ventilator of mines, and employed a jet of high pressure steam to give motion to the column of air in his up-cast shafts. Reid's system, which had answered well in the limited space of the temporary House of Commons, occupied after the fire at the Houses of Parliament until the new Palace at Westminster was ready to receive them, broke down in the larger building, and Gurney had been called in to see if he could improve matters.

Finding that I knew something of the principles on which he acted, he wanted me to be examined as a scientific witness before the Committee of the House of Commons which was sitting on the question of ventilation, which I naturally refused to do. But I did assist him in some experiments at the House, and went with him on this occasion. He had the Speaker's order to admit himself and a friend to see everything connected with the ventilation, but Dr. Reid was furious at being interfered with, and said he would not allow another professional engineer to see his mode of working the ventilation. The Speaker's order was produced, and I calmed Reid's apprehensions by telling him I was not a rival. Gurney begged me to go alone with Reid's foreman, who explained that the floor and ceiling of the house were divided into squares, and that any one of them could be at pleasure made the inlet for fresh air, or the outlet for the foul air. I asked to be taken at once to the supposed inlet for fresh air, which was in the ceiling, and bending over it was nearly suffocated by the blast of foul air issuing from it. Then to the outlet, where, on the contrary, the fresh air was going in. This was enough, and I reported the result to Gurney, and then went to dinner at Sir Charles Fellowes's, the discoverer of the Lycian Marbles now in the British Museum, where we met Sir George Staunton, Owen, Edward Forbes, Hooker, and the Barlows.

59 Montagu Square,<br>5th April 1852.

My dear E.—Many thanks for your kind thought of me on Saturday. The birthdays and all other anniversaries seem to come round faster and faster as one grows older, and the love of those who remember their recurrence is all the more dear, as it must every year become more rare.

Such things are only remembered by very early friends, whose number cannot be increased. I have lately been looking into the present state of the Mormonite question. Very tiresome and tedious on the whole, very humiliating and very shocking in some of its parts, but presenting an amount of vigorous enterprise and of success in the propagation of their opinions which makes it rather a serious affair. I doubt whether they will take permanent root in Europe, except perhaps as emigration agents. But in America the prospect of a new State claiming to be a Theocracy, and disposed to treat their neighbours as the Jews did the Canaanites, is full of wonder and alarming interest.—Yours affectionately, W. F. P.

London, 30*th April* 1852.

Dear E.—You want to know what good Lord Derby's government has done. It has already elevated the standard of political honour and morality to a height unknown for years, and I trust it will make the administration of this country what it ought to be, and what all government, from that of the smallest nursery to that of the greatest empire, must be if it is to be good for anything—namely, a wise and firm, although responsible and liberal control of the affairs of the country; not a mere organ to receive impressions, invite opinions, and to exist by favouring one set of clamourers in turn after another, without the power of guiding, or the heart and courage to govern at all, but, on the contrary, itself governed by every turn of faction, and dismayed and perplexed by every difficulty in its way. Do you remember Wordsworth's lines?—

" We shall exult when they who rule this land
    Are men who hold its many blessings dear ;

> Wise, upright, valiant—not a servile band
> . . . to judge of danger which they fear,
> And honour which they do not understand."—

Yours affectionately, W. F. P.

*8th May.*—To Cambridge to spend two or three days with Thompson, now Greek Professor, at his rooms in Trinity. I suppose it was the first occasion of a lady staying in College, except at the Lodge. But he had one of the fine sets of rooms approached by the gateway under the clock tower, which were in all ways comfortable and commodious. We had for diversion while our host was engaged, a bagful of English poems competing for the Chancellor's medal to read, as to which no confidences can be divulged.

*22d May.*—To a morning lecture of Faraday's. He called nitrogen an unpresuming and negative element—indifferent to electricity—and perhaps not a simple body.

*16th June.*—C. C. S. dinner at Blackwall—F. Lushington presided.

*2d August.*—Went over Babbage's workshops, in which the difference calculating engine had been constructed, and saw the drawings on paper for the analytical engine, which superseded the former, but the construction of which was never commenced. It was a strange fortune for a man to have eclipsed himself, as it were, in this way; and the deserted workbenches, lathes, and tools presented a dreary and melancholy spectacle. There was no branch of science to which Babbage did not make some valuable addition, or upon which he did not throw some light. But for his engrossment by the calculating engines, and all the troubles and annoyances to which they gave rise, Babbage would probably have made great discoveries, and would have been eminent as a physicist. Now his name is chiefly known as that of an inventor struggling with the government of the day for recognition and reward, or rather for payment and assistance, and for his squabbles with other men of science. He was very generous to the Swedish inventors of a calculating machine, founded on his own, but with practical improvements, and assisted them in every way. Evening at Forster's, where were Dr. Elliotson, R. Browning, Broderip, Kenyon, W. S. Landor.

*St. Julian's, 2d September.*—Mr. Herries thinks that Lord Melville appropriated the

£10,000 for which he was impeached for a private purpose, meaning to restore it again, and that it was restored. This was also the opinion of Sir Robert Peel. Pitt suffered much from a conviction of his friend's delinquency. Lord Melville died at the house of the Lord President Blair, to which he had gone to attend the President's funeral, which was to take place the next day. Lord Melville died suddenly in the night, and on his table was found a letter written by him describing the funeral as if it had already taken place.

*8th September.*—To Lyme Regis, to which we were attracted in order to do homage to the memory of Jane Austen, and to discover, if we could, the very spot on the Lower Cobb where Louisa Musgrove met with her accident in *Persuasion*. We found comfortable quarters over the shop of the principal bookseller, who wanted to know if I was the author of *The Course of Time*, and afterwards mentioned our arrival to some of the residents, who came to call on us in a very friendly and unworldly manner. The varied scenery of the country around gave plenty of occasion for walks and sketching, in which one difficulty was to match from the colour-box the deep blue of the sea. The scars of the great landslip at Dowlands were not yet quite healed, and this was a favourite resort, as were Uplyme and Charmouth; and there were drives to Ford Abbey, and walks to Sidmouth, Seaton, and Beer. One day I walked to Whitchurch Canonicorum, and was shown over the church by Palmer, the parson (the author of *Origines Liturgicæ*).

*18th November.*—We saw the funeral procession of the Duke of Wellington pass along Piccadilly from the rooms of Charles Herries, over Truefitt's shop. I had a ticket for St. Paul's, and might perhaps have got there in time to see also the ceremony inside, but did not try to do so.

*28th December.*—Letter from Chapman and Hall finally accepting the publication of my translation of the *Divina Commedia*, on the so-called half-profits arrangement, the iniquity and delusion of which I did not so well understand then as I do now. They brought out the book, however, in a very handsome manner, with fine paper and type, and went to considerable expense for the illustrations, prepared on my suggestion by George Scharf, and for their being cut on wood by the eminent brothers Dalziel. It had a fair sale; but some years afterwards one of those things happened which could not have taken place in any other business but that of publishers. They disposed of the remaining stock, which was, of course, half mine, without consulting me, and for a short time the book was to be had at a very reduced price. It is now difficult to procure, and, as I am told, has become a scarce book.

St. Julian's, *29th December* 1852.

My dear E.—Two notes from you have helped the pleasure of being here. One of them did not arrive exactly as you intended on the morning of Christmas day, but it did not lose any of its value on that account. I am glad to know that you have been sharing in the golden certainties of Australia. What a strange revolution in the value of property! I wish that all freaks of fortune may be equally beneficial to you. The weather since we came here has been extraordinary; and the leafless landscape, with the thermometer at 55°, and the greens of the grass and the shrubs as bright as in the spring, is peculiarly beautiful. There is, indeed, almost more colour than at other times— the woods are full of warm red and purple tints, the old walls and roofs of cottages are richly varied by lichens and mosses of the brightest hue; and in the garden-beds are left plenty of fuchsias, salvias, hydrangeas, and other plants in flower. Yesterday evening for a few minutes before sunset the effect was most gorgeous; the exceeding beauty and delicacy of the complex tracery of branches was seen distinctly to the smallest twig in the nearer trees. There was almost the same feeling of admiration for successful elaboration and perfect execution that might have been felt in looking at a picture of the subject. The children have been much enjoying their time here, and the variety of company in the drawing-room and housekeeper's room is useful in diverting F——'s attention from books, in which he is apt to get too much immersed.—Yours affectionately, W. F. P.

LONDON, 17*th February* 1853.

DEAR E.—We were on Saturday at Madame Bunsen's, at your uncle's old house in Carlton Terrace, now bought for the Prussian minister at the Court of St. James. There is a colossal bust of Frederick the Great on the staircase. I suppose it has the largest cocked-hat and feathers which ever figured in a work of art. The floor of the long drawing-room is inlaid with polished wood, and has no carpet. Altogether the house is now very handsome, and all in good taste. We had some people dining with us last week, and among them a very charming and clever person,—the E. V. B. of *Child's Play*,—which you may have seen in Montagu Square. She is Mrs. Boyle,—a daughter-in-law of Lord Cork,—and her husband has a living near Frome, where Mr. Bennett is playing his fantastic tricks before high heaven ; and we are much delighted with her, and regret that we are not likely, from her residence in the country, ever to see much of her. We met her at Eastlake's ; but I fancy she and J—— knew something of each other beforehand, by Boxall's description of one to the other of them.

On Monday Master Walter will be three years old, and is

going to entertain some of his young friends with a conjuror.—Yours affectionately, W. F. P.

*18th April.*—Evening at Mrs. Carrick Moore's in Clarges Street. Faraday, Babbage, Lyells, Mrs. Jameson, Lady Eastlake, John Murray, Sir C. Fellowes, etc.

*19th April.*—Evening at Chauncey Hare Townsend's. Dickens, Bunsen, F. Stone, Millais, Derwent Coleridges, Samuel Laurence, Dr. Elliotson, Leach, etc.

*23d April* 1853.

DEAR E.—You say that the Irish take a great interest in the Jews. I wonder if this feeling is as old as Cromwell's time, and whether it prompted him to his scheme of selling Ireland to the Jews, and letting them build a national temple in Dublin. Generally speaking, one would say that the interest taken *in* the Jews anywhere is not so great as the interest taken *by* them, and perhaps the want of scope for the latter development of interest in Ireland may leave room for the former.—Yours affectionately, W. F. P.

*15th May.* — With Boxall to Marochetti's studio, in Onslow Square. Saw his figure of Prince Arthur and head of Lord Lansdowne. Introduced to Count Massimo d'Azeglio, who was painting in one of the rooms.

*23d May.*—At dinner W. B. Donne, Spedding, Lear, Copley Fielding.

LONDON, 31*st* *May* 1853.

DEAR E.—We had L—— O—— dining with us the other day. He does not seem to find Scots Law more to his taste than our English commodity in that line. He was full of "turning tables," and a great believer in all the foolish things that are current about them. Perhaps you would like to hear the most wonderful story on this subject. It was during the late cold weather, when everybody was suffering from influenza, that a table surrounded by a circle of devotees was so much affected by their "vital influence" that it actually gave a loud sneeze, and another table in the same room immediately said, "God bless you!"

One day last week we were at a very pretty entertainment at St. Mark's, Chelsea. It was the birthday of Christabel Coleridge, and was celebrated by a child's party in the garden. Fairy wands with flowers had been prepared for the children, and they ran about in groups, or one by one, like little Arcadians. Then there were many of the red-coated boys from the Military School, with their juvenile band to play marches and country-dance tunes, while the boys and girls made merry round a May-pole. It was a real children's party, with nothing unchildlike, or which children could not or might not enjoy. F—— was much delighted.—Yours affectionately,            W. F. P.

*3d June.*—Presided as one of the Masters at the examination of articled clerks for admission as attorneys at the Law Institution, and dined with the Council. I was much dissatisfied with the system under which the examination was at this time conducted, when the candidates were either simply passed or plucked, and there were no means of recognising the credit due to those who had distinguished themselves by their answers. I wrote to Lord Campbell, as Lord Chief Justice, on the subject, and received an answer favourable to the adoption of honorary distinctions, and this was the beginning of the award of honours in these examinations, which has since prevailed. At this or on some subsequent occasion I got from one candidate for admission to practice as an attorney as answer to the question, "Can a minor sue, or be sued, on a promise to marry?"—"No, because marriage is not a necessary." To the question, "What is a charter-party?" came for answer, "A charter-party is the party who charters a ship."

LONDON, 5*th July* 1853.

MY DEAR E.—On Friday we are to have the pleasure of a visit to Macready for a week. His patient endurance of the greatest sorrows that can befall a man has more than ever endeared him to us, and we hope that our visit may help to dispel some of the sadness which must always remain in his house.

Touching the "moving tables," I suppose that Faraday's letter printed in the *Times* has satisfied all sensible people, although I do see that a philosopher in Southwark thinks his experiments "*unfair.*" For the other folly of the day which you mention, I wonder at you writing of it so seriously, for I have always thought the spirit-rapping business one of the most culpable and degrading impostures ever practised upon the superstitious and weak-minded, and having upon its front all the *indicia* of fraud. Conceive the abominable imposture of a supposed conversation with Sir John Franklin! I want no other spirits to assist me in the comprehension of the mystery of "rapping" than the spirit of making money, which has been potent to transfer some of that master-mover of all things from the pockets of some fools to those of the pretenders to the art of conversing with the dead. As to the particular explanation of how the fraud is practised, I am no more bound to be able precisely to explain it than how M. Houdin, or any other amuser of the public, contrives to pour champagne, port, and sherry out of the same bottle, or to extract an inexhaustible supply of bouquets from the inside of a hat. No doubt it involves some clever contrivances, enormous impudence, and a good deal of close observation of character and of what goes on in the room, and, above all, a boundless reliance upon the gullibility of mankind, which is the grand article in the stock in trade of all charlatans—political, legal, psychological, or otherwise—and upon the chapter of accidents and lucky coincidences, which probably furnish them with their most successful hits. I have not attended, and do not mean to attend, any of these performances, which, besides their folly and fraud, are said to be the dullest affairs possible.—Yours affectionately,

W. F. P.

In the summer we paid a second visit to Macready at Sherborne, and passed the greater part of the autumn vacation in Cumberland. We began with a visit to Mrs. John Spedding at Oakfield, and thence passed to Mirehouse, then belonging to Tom Spedding, and afterwards went into a little hired cottage at Applethwaite, nestled among the slopes of Skiddaw, and from which there is a fine view, across Derwent Water, of Borrowdale and the mountains beyond the lake.  It was an extremely wet season, but we managed to get some good walks and drives, and I made the ascent of Scaw Fell, getting a glorious tea-dinner at Mr. Fisher's, of Seatoller, on our return.  Climbing among the English mountains is a small affair, as to heights and distances, when compared with similar work on the Alps, but it has its advantages.  The scenery is beautiful, and great changes in it are quickly attainable.  Everything can be done between breakfast and dinner, and there is risk enough to require caution.  The frequent wet weather is a drawback, but without rain the Lake Country loses much of its charm.  The streams are dry and silent, the water in the falls merely slinks among the rocks, distant views are destroyed, and it is not difficult to get reconciled even to an almost perpetual rainfall.

It was during this year that my second son, W——, learned to read in a singular manner. His mother used to read out to him for half an hour every day, before dressing for dinner, from Longfellow's "Hiawatha." At the close of the reading he would always ask for more, and his mother would reply, "I cannot read any more now, but if you like to take the book and look at the words as I have read them to you, you may do so." To this suggestion the boy eagerly agreed, and by this process, at the end of a fortnight, he could read the whole of the poem with ease. He was then five years old, but did not know his letters. This is a curious instance of what may be done by the enthusiasm of the learner to help a teacher.

*11th October.*—Dined with Brookfields. Mr. Hallam (Mrs. B.'s uncle), Alfred and Frederick Tennyson.

*31st December.*—Translation of the *Divina Commedia* published.

*1st February* 1854.—Dined with Boxall. Richmond came in, and, talking of the effect of dress in portraits, he remarked that the ruff round the neck, as worn in the time of Queen

Elizabeth, sets off the face, like the white mount of a drawing.

*14th February.*—Dinner at home. Lady Eastlake, Herman Merivales, Alfords, Kenneth Macaulays, Groves, Charles Herries.

*15th March.*—To Olympic Theatre. Robson in *To Oblige Benson;* Mrs. Wigan in *The Bengal Tiger;* Wigan and Miss Horton in *The First Night.* Robson was now beginning a career which was only too brief. His intensity was wonderful, but his efforts were incapable of being long maintained. For a minute or two in the burlesque of *Medea* he seemed almost equal to Ristori. His range, however, was limited, and he had reached his highest mark before failing health obliged him to leave the stage. Mrs. Wigan was a great artist, knowing her business thoroughly, and with real passion in her, to which she was qualified to give the best expression. In *Still Waters Run Deep* she was unrivalled. Wigan was a good actor, and has not in his own line of parts been equalled since. Miss Horton, now and for long Mrs. German Reed, was a delightful singer, and was full of charm and of great intelligence. Her Ariel, and Fool in

*King Lear*, under Macready's management, can never be forgotten by those who saw her in those parts.

*1st April.*—To Sherborne, to give a lecture on Dante at the Literary Institution, in which Macready took so much interest, which has been told of by my wife in her *Macready As I Knew Him*—a book which exhibits him to more truth and advantage than he has shown himself in his own *Reminiscences and Diaries*. In the following week Forster gave a lecture on Strafford, which we remained to hear. Afterwards Katie Macready came to stay with us for some days.

*13th May.*—At dinner Boxall and Tyndall. I had made Tyndall's acquaintance at one of the soirees given by the Earl of Rosse, as President of the Royal Society, at his house in Connaught Place. He had come up from Manchester to give us a lecture at the Royal Institution, and he, being then almost a stranger in London, and standing alone in the room, was pointed out to Sir Charles Fellowes and myself, who were talking together. We were at the time both managers of the Institution, and finding no one to introduce us, we agreed to introduce each other, which we did. This was the commencement of a long and affectionate friendship, of equal profit and delight to my wife, my sons, and to myself.

*20th May.*—Dined Forster's. Alfred Tennyson, Boxall, Maclise, Spedding.

*3d June.*—To French play. *Jean au Printemps, Le Mariage Forcé, La Joie fait Peur*, with Regnier, Lafont, Madame Allan, and Mdlle. Luther. Madame Allan was an actress of much distinction and of great tragic power, who would have undoubtedly taken the place she deserved but for the disadvantage of her short stature and plain wide face. She held a high position, nevertheless, wherever she appeared. Mdlle. Luther was a beautiful girl of extraordinary sensibility, but unfortunately died at an early age.

*13th June.* — Dined Dickens's. Macready and his daughter Katie, Forster, James White, Scott Russell, Chauncey Townsend, Dr. Elliotson, Miss Boyle. In the evening Miss Burdett Coutts. Played at games.

*14th June.*—Evening at Lady Eastlake's. Story of Edwin Landseer being presented to the King of Portugal, and his majesty saying,

"Ah! I am glad to see you. I always like beasts."

ALBION HOTEL,<br>BROADSTAIRS, 21st June 1854.

MY DEAR E.—You will be surprised at the above date and place, but need not be alarmed, although we are certainly here by the counsel of our Æsculapius. Little W—— has been unwell with some derangement of his small interior, and Headland has strongly advised sea air, both for him and F——. J—— is always the better for it, and I have been able to arrange a short absence from official duty, and shall be glad to get a break after two months of London and work, and to lay in a stock of health which I hope may last until the long vacation begins. So I gave up a Cambridge dinner to be held at Greenwich to-day, the price of which, by-the-bye, just paid our coming here. We took the boat to Margate yesterday, and here we are for a week under the hospitable care of Mr. Ballard, at one of whose open windows I am writing, with a most beautiful shifting scene before me of sun and shadow, and green and purple tints upon the sea. The boys are already better, and of course are busily engaged upon some of the never-ending, still-beginning excavations upon the sands, and in throwing up works, and sinking cuttings of a less definite kind than I should have expected from F——'s precise habits, for I cannot make out whether they are the bastions of Silestria, or the Russian lines, or railway undertakings, or canals. To-morrow, perhaps, they will get more into shape. To-day they are what old Coleridge might have called "abstract fruitions of sand digging." You know this place and its grumbling ways, and you will not be amazed to hear that Broadstairs is going to be ruined this year more than ever. What with income-tax, high prices, and people going abroad, no one is expected to come here, and those who do come are not to spend any money. As for Margate, it is a doomed city as much as if Jonas had gone out and denounced it. Indeed, the population who received the steamboat on the pier was not larger than the arrivals by it, and if we had been an invading force I think we could have easily overpowered the small numbers who held the pier. Broadstairs, therefore, complacently hands over Margate and Ramsgate to utter bankruptcy. For itself, thanks to the greater respectability, or rather the "*goodness*" of the families who have nothing from the butcher but "the primest joints" (and I suppose there can be no higher standard of "goodness" and "respectability"), Broadstairs hopes to struggle on, only with rather more ruin than usual—but, so far as we are concerned, the ruin is more likely to be on our side.—Yours affectionately,

W. F. P.

*27th June.*—Dined with Chauncey Hare Townsend, Norfolk Street, Park Lane. Bulwer Lytton and his son, Barlows, Derwent Coleridges, Miss Burdett Coutts, Lady Goderich.

*29th June.*—To F. D. Maurice's third lecture at Willis's Rooms, on learning and working. It is a course of lectures to introduce a scheme for a college for working-men, in which gentlemen are to be the teachers.

*3d July.*—Dined with Derwent Coleridges

at St. Mark's College, Chelsea. Was much surprised to find certain reverend gentlemen doubting the lawfulness of assisting Turkey in a war with Russia, because the Turks are not Christians. I never heard such an objection made against helping animals in trouble, why then should it be made in the case of human beings who are in need of assistance?

*4th July.* — Master's Club dinner at the Trafalgar, Greenwich.

*11th July.* — To Crystal Palace at Sydenham, driving down by the road. Certainly very beautiful, and will be more so as the plants grow. In the different Fine Art Courts, the colouring is overdone. The decorators seem to have gone mad with love for paint. The Greek Court, with its noble casts from the greatest statues of antiquity, is the finest thing. The savages are trumpery. But the wonderful fact of all is the eating and drinking; not 40 but 400 may be seen feeding like one, and for 2s., neither more nor less, you get your fill of cold viands.

*13th July.* — Dinner at Eastlake's. Cockerell, the architect, Layard, Sir E. Landseer, John Murray, Waagen. All the artists condemn the excessive use of colour in the Crystal Palace. Layard, however, said that the Nineveh Court was not bright enough to please him.

*17th July.*—At dinner, Macready, Forster, Spedding, Venables. The Duke of Newcastle has given young Macready a Ceylon appointment.

*10th August.*—Dined with Boxall. Copley Fielding came in afterwards. He is always charming and good company.

*11th August.*—Professor Tyndall dined with us, and brought a magnetic toy of mice for W——, and another of two men tumbling upstairs to illustrate the principle of the centre of gravity. This toy used to come from China, but now comes from the headquarters of toydom in Germany. Tyndall is full of English poetry, and seems to like talking about it more than of his science. He now stands at the Royal Institution as the probable successor to Davy and Faraday, and I expect will not prove unworthy of them.

*16th August.*—To Putney. Found Miss Julia Moore at the station in a carriage with Lady Bell. Pleasant drive round Richmond

Park. On return found Sir Charles Lyell and Lady Lyell, who dined. Mr. Moore is a remarkable man. He is the brother of Sir John Moore of Corunna, and now ninety-two years old; deaf and very blind, but able to enjoy familiar society, taking an interest in all that is going on; kind and considerate to the people around him, and able to derive his chief pleasure from chess. Mrs. Moore is the daughter of Henderson the actor, who, though a younger man, was a contemporary of Garrick's. She has often sat upon Dr. Johnson's knee. A story was told of an American lady-writer, who, meaning to pay a compliment to Sir John Herschel on being lately introduced to him in London, said, "You are quite famous in America. My little books have carried your name through all the States."

*22d August.*—By South Western Railway to Poole, and thence posting to Bournemouth, where both hotels were full and no obvious signs of lodgings to be had. The place is surrounded inland for three or four miles by flat heaths, varied by thick plantations of fir. The little town itself is composed of villa-like houses, reminding one of some parts of St.

John's Wood, and a few shops. There is no sea-side walk, no pier, and no shipping, and an air of novelty and dependence on distant markets for all necessaries. So we went on, or rather backwards, to Christ Church, where was a good old-fashioned inn, overlooking the fine church, and with a distant view of the Isle of Wight Needles, across green meadows and a winding stream, one of the many Avons in England; and here we stayed for the night.

*23d August.*—Saw interior of the church, which is full of interest. A fine Anglo-Norman nave, restored thirty years ago; a late decorated chancel, and a very late perpendicular lady-chapel—all large. Just inside the West door is a monument to Shelley, bearing also the names of his wife and of his mother-in-law, Mrs. Godwin, *née* Wollstonecraft. It has been recently erected by the present Sir Percy Shelley, now living in the neighbourhood.

There is also a touching group by Flaxman, to the memory of Lord Malmesbury's mother, but unfortunately not in marble. Many old tombs, monuments, and chapels; and we greeted kindly the hedge-hogs in the armorial bearings of the Malmesbury family, whose name is Harris—a corruption from Herries, as that is from the old Italian Erizzo, which furnishes the Rizzo, or hedge-hog. The modern Venetian branch add an E to complete the name in their coat-of-arms. On other shields appears an heraldic rebus on the name Harris—a hare holding in her mouth the letter S—Hare-S.

Post back to the railway at Poole, and thence by rail to Dorchester, and read in the *Times* the account of the taking of Bomarsund. Post to Weymouth; much disappointed with the place. Conceive a mile of Baker Street houses of the dingiest hue, arranged in a semicircle round a land-locked bay of dull sea, a row of bathing machines, the biggest of which bears the inscription: " The machine of that good king, George III., the friend of the poor, and patron of Weymouth ;" a statue of the same monarch upon a pedestal so large and so shaped that it looks like a figure upon a French clock, and you have a complete knowledge of Weymouth. So, after a short stroll on the esplanade and dining at an hotel, we took carriage, and by nine o'clock found ourselves in Lyme Regis again. W—— was taken out a perfect lump of sleep, and all the bustle of being carried into the Cups Inn, and being put to bed, did not wake him.

# CHAPTER II

## "FORTUNIO" AT TAVISTOCK HOUSE

*8th January* 1855.—To Dickens's, Tavistock House, to see a performance of an abridged version of Planché's *Fortunio*, in which the parts were chiefly taken by himself and his children. Dickens appeared in the bills as Mr. Passé. They were magnificently printed, some on white satin. Afterwards dancing and supper.

*18th January.*—Dine Kenyon's. Fanny Kemble, Forster, Henry Reeve, Harness, Hardwicke, Mrs. Procter.

*1st March.*—Elected one of the auditors for the ensuing year at the General Court of the Equitable Life Assurance Society.

*12th March.*—Dine with Crabbe Robinson, the Dousterswivel of early days. Met Boxall, Donne, Harness, Dr. Skey.

*14th March.*—Was elected a member of the General Committee of the Royal Literary Fund.

*28th March.*—Dined with B. L. Chapman at the Blue Posts, Cork Street. Monteith, Venables, Garden, Brookfield, W. Macpherson. There were marrow-bones towards the end of a very abundant dinner, and some one remarked that this was heaping *Ossa* on Pelion.

London, *4th April* 1855.

Dear E.—I have been lately reading Trench's little books, which I daresay you know. *The Lessons in Proverbs*, *The Study of Words*, and *English Past and Present*, which last is recent, and, on the whole, perhaps the most interesting. All, however, are suggestive of much more than is actually set forth in them, and deserve the extensive popularity which they enjoy. Of new books I really know none of value. The circulating library and book-club system enables publishers to bring out a certain class of works with a prospect of profit; but of these nine-tenths are, like the razors in the old story, only made to sell, and, having gone their round, read or not read, nobody cares or wishes to hear anything more about them. I was put, at the last meeting, on the Committee of the Literary Fund, and was equally surprised and amused at some of the people who claim relief as literary persons; only one must not talk of being amused when engaged in the business of relieving distress. In truth, much of the so-called literature now produced is rather damaging to the cause of real literature. Unless the increase of readers is overtaken by an extension of real education, the mischief will go on increasing. How few people look at a book requiring any exercise of thought or attention! The appetite is fed on kickshaws and trifles, and an unwholesome course of diet must operate injuriously upon the constitution.—Yours affectionately,

W. F. P.

*16th April.*—To Bricklayers' Arms Station with tickets from James Byng to see the arrival of Louis Napoleon and the French Empress in London. At dinner W. H. Thompson, Spedding, Edward Fitzgerald.

LONDON, *26th June* 1855.

DEAR E.—We have had dining with us Lacaita, and I am glad to have made his acquaintance. He is a Neapolitan gentleman formerly an advocate at Naples, and the widower of a Scottish lady (Carmichael), now resident wholly in England, not exactly a political refugee, but of too enlightened opinions to make his own country an agreeable place for him. He is an accomplished scholar, and professes Italian at the Ladies' College in Harley Street. He gave a Friday evening lecture on Dante at the Royal Institution, in which he praised my translation highly—a tribute the more valuable perhaps as I was not then personally known to him.—Yours affectionately,

W. F. P.

*20th June.*—Dined with the C. C. S. at the Star and Garter, Richmond—a better place than the houses at Blackwall or Greenwich, where the dinner has been formerly held. It affords a pleasant stroll in the Park, such as I had with Venables before dinner. Milnes brought me home.

*30th June.*—Called on Willes at his chambers in the Temple to congratulate him on his appointment as a judge in the Common Pleas, in succession to Maule. He showed me his fee-book for 1854, with a total of more than six thousand guineas, so that he loses income by his promotion to the bench.

*15th July.*—Dined with Brookfields at Mortlake. Henry Taylor, W. H. Thompson, Alfred Wigans.

The autumn was partly spent in a visit to Robert Hildyard, at Shanklin, in the Isle of Wight. Hildyard told a good electioneering story. Lord Stormont's agent at a Norwich election found that an old friend and supporter had taken £4 from the other side to vote against him. He dilated to him upon the wickedness of changing sides, and added that he was a great fool too, for that he would have had £5 if he had stuck to his principles. The inconstant voter was penitent, and the agent went on to say, " But it's not too late for you to do the right thing. Give me that four pounds, and here's a five pound for you," which was a good stroke of business for his employers. We afterwards took a house of our own at Ventnor, where we saw a good deal of James White, author of more than one play, and of some of the best things that have appeared in *Blackwood's Magazine*. Here we heard the painful news of the death of Henry Lushington in Paris, on 11th August. One day we drove to Freshwater, where Tennyson had not long taken up his abode at Ffaringford, and spent the evening with him and his wife. He read us out part of " Maud," not then published, and before we left them to go to our quarters at Plumbly's Hotel, we were taken upstairs to see the beautiful sight of their two handsome boys, Hallam and Lionel, asleep in bed. We spent some hours the next day at Ffaringford, and had the rest of " Maud " read to us in the garden ; took an early dinner with the Tennysons, and drove back to Ventnor.

There was a striking illumination of the cliffs with Bengal lights at Bonchurch on the anniversary of the battle of Alma, to celebrate the fall of Sebastopol, which was not enhanced by a simultaneous display of fireworks. After our return to London we paid another visit to Macready at Sherborne.

*11th October.*—Dinner to Thackeray at the London Tavern on the occasion of his going to lecture in the United States. There were sixty people, and Dickens was in the chair. Neither of the two principal speeches was very felicitous. I sat between Douglas Jerrold and Joseph Parkes, and found the old lawyer and politician the better company of the two, with all his recollections and varied knowledge of life. In the bill of fare there was turtle soup *à la* " Hobson Newcome" and *à la* "bon voyage;" there were omelettes *à la* "Becky Sharp," and a salmi *à la* "Fotheringay."

*19th December.*—Dined Eastlake's. Mulready, Webster, Ward, Cope, Marshall, Knight, and all painters except Panizzi and myself.

*21st December.*—Dined with Milnes. Sir Colin Campbell, Colonel Sterling, Sir Francis Doyle, Horace Mansfield, Brookfield, Cunningham, John Mitchell, Kemble, W. Vernon Harcourt, Captain Burton, Kinglake, Stephen Spring Rice, Henry Phillips.

59 Montagu Square,
22d *February* 1856.

My dear E.—We went the Sunday before last to St. Philip's Church in Regent Street, where Mr. Bellew is preaching and making a sensation. The sermon was certainly a striking one, both in manner and matter. He has formerly taken lessons in elocution from Macready, who asked us to go and hear him. Occasionally the recollections of the master disturbed the effects intended to be produced by the pupil, but he certainly deserves his popularity. Mr. Bellew has a remarkable head of black hair; old Mr. Repton, who read prayers, has a white and bald pate. It was little W———'s first time at church, and when we came out Bobo, who is near-sighted, raised a question whether the same gentleman had read prayers and preached, and gave his own opinion that it was the same. W———, who had noticed the change from the surplice to the black gown, and who modestly thought himself unfit to decide the point, and perhaps was uncertain whether there might not have been the same change in the head as in the gowns, said, "But when he was downstairs he had a white head."

I have been reading Napoleon's letters to Joseph in the English translation, which is extremely well done. They give an additional touch of great value to the known character of the man, and are full of the sort of wisdom that was in him—thoroughly unscrupulous, but untiring in its vigilance and perseverance to gain its end. His expressions of contempt for the French in his confidential communications with his Corsican brother are amusing. Well, indeed, might he despise the people of whom he was making tools for his own selfish aggrandisement.

I wonder whether you ever came across Marivaux's *Vie*

*de Marianne*, which I have been lately enjoying. It is the book which really is entitled to be called the first of the modern novels. Beautifully written, with the most delicate delineations of character, and a story of common life. I think Miss Burney must have known it before she wrote *Evelina*, parts of which seem to me to have been adapted from it, and every novel written since has, consciously or unconsciously, been indebted to it. There is a description of the love of excitement and cruel indifference to the sufferings of others, which was fearfully verified fifty years afterwards in the scenes of the first Revolution, although it is introduced *apropos* to a squabble between a hackney coachman and his fare. There is a discussion on the essentials of good manners and conversation which exhausts the subject, and there is a very clever, true, and amusing account of the reasons why stupid people get the credit of being good, with little enough claim to it.

*1st March* 1856.

DEAR E.—We had a remarkable lecture last night at the R. I. from Professor Thomson, formerly of Cambridge, and now of Glasgow. He derives all the motive power on the earth's surface, in the first instance, from the heat of the sun, which he describes as a force capable of accumulation in a latent form, and of development into activity in various ways. For instance, is a horse in a mill, or drawing a carriage, or otherwise, the source of power? How did the animal acquire his muscular strength? From his food, which was once grass or corn growing by the stimulus of the sun's light and heat. Is the source of power a steam-engine? It is kept in motion by the expansion of steam, caused by the heat of burning coal. This coal was once living vegetable matter, also, as in the case of the horse's fodder, grown by the agency of the sun's heat. And so on. The speculation is ingenious and true, if confined to the sun's heat acting on the earth, but there is no more reason for assuming heat in general to be the primordial cause of motion than any other of the correlative forces—electricity, galvanism, or motive force itself, with which it is now known to be convertible. Starting from any one of these, it can always be transformed into manifestations of some or one of the others, and it would be an arbitrary proceeding to give any priority to one over the others. Besides, the theory altogether omits the force of gravity, which hitherto has not been brought into such intimate relations with the rest as they enjoy among themselves—that is, it fails to show how the force of gravity depends on the sun's heat. Nevertheless, in more advanced stages of knowledge this, too, may turn out to be true.

We are casting about to get a week's country air at Easter, and shall probably go to Tunbridge Wells. It would be better to postpone this if we could until the hotter weather begins to make a change from London more desirable; but we must take it when we can get it, and I know of no pleasanter place within easy reach of London than the Wells. Reigate is charming for a day or two, but it has no resources in the event of rainy days.

You may be certain there will be peace. Russia wants it, France wants it, and, of course, England—though quite able to carry on the war, which the other powers are not—will be glad of it.

*17th March* 1856.

DEAR E.—What you say about Sydney Smith's letters is true. They are not always equal to his conversational reputation. But who can always be witty? and why should the survivors of celebrated men publish all their correspondence, as it is now so much the fashion to do? It leads to the printing of a great many dull letters, which only injure the reputation of the writer, if it is to be affected by them at all.

Macaulay has lately received from the Longmans a cheque for £20,000 on account of his share of the profits of the last two volumes of his *History*. It is the largest sum ever paid to an author, and it is said that the publishers have no reason to complain of their portion of the spoil.

We had a pleasant dinner at home last Wednesday, comprising the Barlows, the Derwent Coleridges, John Murray, the Dean of Hereford (of educational note), Lady James (Sir Walter being absent at the Kent Assizes), and Charles and Izzy Herries. Two or three men came in the evening, of whom one was Lacaita, who is to give a lecture on Dante this week at the London Institution, for which I have lent him some of my editions and commentaries.

*20th March.*—To Tunbridge Wells. Miss W—— had taken good lodgings for us in Clarence Terrace, in a sheltered position, but overlooking the common. It was cold during all our stay, and the country not yet got up for the reception of company—the best things locked up, the covers on the furniture, fires not lighted, so to speak—yet the change from London was useful. Truly a very early and cold Easter. Winter's carriage stopping the way, in spite of the cries of "Miss Spring coming out!"

*21st, Good Friday.*—To the church at the top of the town. Mr. H—— preached, and for all he said to the contrary the congregation might have gone away and violated every precept of the Decalogue. I was told this was always the case in his sermons—the incumbent wishing to set his face against "works."

*23d, Sunday.*—To the chapel by the Pantiles. This, I suppose, was built when the Wells became fashionable in Charles II.'s time, and is dedicated to King Charles the Martyr. It is a square room, with a handsome panelled ceiling, filled with movable seats below, and a gallery round three sides, all in dark oak. Its arrangements would shock the modern ecclesiological coxcombs. I liked its simplicity and convenient adaptation to the purposes of a church. A good service and a plain sermon from Mr. Pope.

*1st April.*—Dined with Forster; met Macready, Maclise, Bellew. A good story was told of modern picture-dealers' frauds. Some years ago Charles Landseer, the brother of Sir Edwin, painted a picture called "Edgehill," which I believe consisted of the figure of a peasant girl, or one or more figures, in the scene of the battle. It was on the wall of the Academy Exhibition, when some one, on the artists' day for varnishing, re-touching, etc., noticed a part which wanted filling in. Sir Edwin good-naturedly said he would put in a couple of dogs on the spot, which he did, of course in a slight manner, and the picture was much improved. The story got wind, and the picture was afterwards sold at a high price on the ground of the dogs by Sir Edwin. Some time afterwards a dealer brought to Sir Edwin a sketch of dogs, and asked him to authenticate it as his. Sir E. said he could not undertake to remember having painted them, but said they looked like his. Lately the present owner of the "Edgehill" picture, a gentleman at Clapham, and who had paid a large price for it, chiefly for the sake of the reputed Sir Edwin's dogs in it, begged of him to come and see it and confirm the tradition. He went, saw the picture, and at once detected what had been done: the dogs had been cut out of the picture, replaced by a bad copy, and no doubt were the dogs (mounted on a fresh canvas) which had been shown to him. This is supposed to be the cleverest case of dog-stealing recorded.

In the evening we saw a series of forty drawings by Maclise from the life of Harold, no doubt suggested by the Bayeux Tapestry.

*2d April.*—Went over Cubitt's works at Pimlico. In one place they were breaking up as old iron the columns designed by Nash for the Regent Street Quadrant—an instance of the mutability of things. A morticing machine, and one for executing mouldings in wood, were curious. All parts of a house are made on the premises—floors and doors, windows, grates, gas-fittings, etc.

*4th April.*—Lacaita called to propose a joint edition of Dante, with notes in English. If Murray will undertake it, which seems not improbable, I should like this, as there is not extant any good edition with reasonable and equally distributed notes, and I have by me a good deal of material.

*Wednesday, 9th April.*—Committee meeting at Literary Fund. Story of George Dyer, the *amicus redivivus* of Elia, who, in a fit of absence, walked out of Lamb's lodgings at Islington into the New River. He was at one time a Baptist minister, and while performing the rite of baptism by total immersion he fell into a reverie, and held an old woman under water until she was drowned.

*Thursday, 10th April.*—Dined with Robert Bell, editor of a current issue of *British Poets* (not the old Bell of that denomination). There was Helen Faucit, the eminent actress, with her husband, Mr. Martin. She is a quiet, pleasant, and very ladylike person. Dr. Mayo, Sir John Forbes, the physician, and Kaye, a friend of Sir George's, known as a writer on Indian affairs.

*11th April.*—Dinner at home. T. F. Ellis, Garden, and others. Some stories were told of bad French. One was the order given to the chambermaid at an hotel to have the sheets well aired, by saying to her, "Mettez les drapeaux au feu." Another was a question put on being shown over a glass-house for raising grapes, "Usez vous aucun feu d'artifice?" and a third, "oreillers" for ear-rings.

*16th April.*—Dined at John Murray's in Albemarle Street. George, Lady Eastlake, Elwin (editor of the *Quarterly*), Babbage, and Mrs. Murray's brother from Edinburgh. The dining-room is on the drawing-room floor, as the ground floor is occupied by "the shop." It is hung with portraits. On the table was a beautiful small silver vase, a present from Lord Byron to old Murray. There are to be articles on Ruskin in the forthcoming *Edinburgh* and *Quarterly*, both condemnatory. It is a pity that persons competent to the task have not before now interfered to prevent so seductive a writer from obtaining any authority in matters of art. He is unprincipled in art, but has been allowed to acquire an influence which has been chiefly for mischief, and it is probably now too late to undo it. After dinner Babbage told some of his favourite stories of successful bank robberies. The associations of the place with the name of our host tempted me to travesty Pope's line—

"How great a burglar was in Babbage lost!"

His main story is of an enormous loss by a Scots bank. A couple of Scots lawyers listened to the story with great composure; but next morning one of them, Murray's brother-in-law, told George, who was sleeping at the house, that most of the interesting facts which gave a zest to the story, and almost made one wish to have been one of the burglars, were not true. I suggested that they had the story from the bank, and that Babbage had it from the burglars, who were likely to know most about it. Saw the original MS. by Scott of his review of the *Life and Works of Home*, the author of *Douglas*, in the *Quarterly*—very legible and distinct, and with very few alterations.

*Friday, 18th April.*— Evening at Royal Institution; lecture by Bence Jones on "Ventilation," founded on some recent inquiries officially made by him into the condition of St. Pancras Workhouse. There was hardly enough of novel matter to justify the choice of the subject. He pointed out the sufficiently obvious truth that the mere statement of the number of cubic feet of air surrounding a person gave no correct indication of good or bad ventilation. The amount of *change* taking place in the surrounding air is the important thing. A man might ultimately die for want of air in the midst of St. Paul's Cathedral if every crevice in the building could be hermetically stopped; for a time must at last arrive when he would have consumed all the oxygen within the walls. On the other hand, a diver, properly supplied with air, may remain as long as he pleases in the narrow compass of his bell or helmet. The only true test, therefore, for sanitary purposes is to ascertain the amount of vitiation of the air in a room by the expired carbonic acid; and the practical value of the lecture consisted in the explanation of various modes in which this measure could be obtained.

*22d April.*—At dinner my father, Charles, Henry, Forster. The Chief Baron offered me a "day-peerage," if one may call it so, in the shape of his ticket for the *Transit* to see the Naval Review the next day with the members of the House of Lords. Fortunately for myself I declined it, and I did not share the troubles of that noble company.

*23d April.*—A holiday for me, as the Courts did not sit on account of the review. Went to the National Gallery to look again at the new Paolo Veronese. It is hardly a first-rate example of the master, and has been cleaned and retouched in places; but one cannot doubt the wisdom of securing it at the price paid.

It is said that the French Government would have given £600 more than we have done.

*24th April.*—The judges who had been to the review the day before, which they did not see, came down to Court in a very bad humour, and said they would never go a-pleasuring any more. Up at 5.30 A.M.; jostled at the Railway Station; detained on the line by the breaking down of a train in front; hustled at Southampton; kept waiting on the quay; badly fed on board; too late to see the Review; fires let out, and no steam when it was time to return; four hours getting from Portsmouth to Southampton; arrived in London at 3 A.M. the next morning; no cabs at the station, etc., etc., etc.

*1st May* 1856.

DEAR E.—You are mistaken in supposing that I am connected with the —— Review. I do happen to know some of those who, as I suppose, contribute to it; but I am not in their councils or confidence, and I would always rather not know whose articles I am reading. Like the rest of the public, I am deluded by the anonymous *we;* and I might not read things so quietly as I do if I knew that it was only my acquaintance A. B., or my friend C. D., or my favourite aversion E. F., whose opinions were in print before me. Hence I am not concerned to meet your comments; but I can forward them, if you please, to the person whom I believe to be the writer of the article which has provoked them, and who is, I daresay, quite open to argument on the alleged simplicities of technical theology, and is no doubt competent to conduct it on that or any other grounds. As far as one of its readers may wish, I would rather the Review kept out of the fray of religious controversy; but as long as there are professed (so called) religious journals, and a (so called) *religious world* (what a contradiction of Christian truth!), it may be necessary for some one occasionally to throw himself in the path of the bullies and hypocrites who abuse the name of religion—to expose their ignorance, rebuke their want of charity, and protest against the bondage in which they would keep their victims. W. F. P.

*29th May* 1856.

DEAR E.—There has been a re-appearance of the sisters of Horace Twiss, the eldest now with brevet ranks as Mrs. Twiss, one talking of dear William's acting (meaning Macready), and the other stoutly holding to the family glories of Uncle Kemble (meaning John K.). There has been for me a magnificent dinner of the directors of the Equitable Insurance Office at the Albion Tavern, given to our president, Sir Charles Morgan, one of those feasts to which it is impossible to do justice, and where one was inclined to dine off a slice of cold beef in perfect despair. There has been a deal of talking and thinking about fireworks and illuminations, and whether to illuminate or not. When I left home this morning there was a modest V in position in front of our balcony, to which the zeal of the boys had added two toy flags, which fluttered in the breeze. George comes up to us to dine and sleep, and I fancy we shall go to Lady Coltman's in Hyde Park Gardens, leave J—— and Bobo there, and then pass into the open park. Poor W—— must stay at home. Hyde Park Gardens is a little too far off, but, on the whole, will not be a bad position. Charles Herries has rooms in Piccadilly facing the Green Park, and close to the space enclosed for the fireworks, but unfortunately all view is cut off by trees and the large shed erected for the occasion. At present the day is cold and cloudy, a duller Queen's birthday than I can remember. It is to be hoped there will be no rain at night.

You have no doubt shared in the general interest in Palmer's trial. His acquittal would indeed have been a great public misfortune and failure of justice. It is remarkable that the case of Mrs. Dove, poisoned by strychnine at Leeds, and no doubt suggested by Palmer's apparent prospect of impunity, should have furnished important evidence towards the conviction of Palmer. The length also to which the surrounding circumstances in evidence ran is a new feature in a criminal trial, and must be considered as owing to the increased publicity now given to facts extrajudicially, and which makes it necessary, for the ends of justice, that they should be also legally brought before the jury. Fifty years ago, I daresay, some of the evidence might have been thought hardly admissible, and would not have been perhaps brought forward.—Yours affectionately,

W. F. P.

*29th May.*—The peace rejoicings. J—— and Bobo to Lady Coltman's house in Hyde Park Gardens, where we mounted to the roof and found Miss Herries and other ladies on chairs in the front gutter, from which, as afterwards appeared, they had an excellent view of the fireworks. George and I went among the people in the Park, and had a good standing place within a few yards of the enclosure. The rockets and other aerial displays were fine, but wanted variety; the wheels and other fixed pieces were not large enough to produce much effect, with the exception of the two fountains of fire at the close, and some mines of squibs. The display lasted so long that our servants, coming out in two detachments, all saw as much as they wanted of it. The rockets, etc., from the Green Park and on Primrose Hill were well seen from Hyde Park, and the finest effect was that of the last blaze in Green Park as seen from Hyde Park. I saw no accident from rocket-sticks, and wonder there were so few reported the next day. Returned to Lady Coltman's, where there was some supper, and then escorted Miss Herries to her resting-place in Norfolk Street, and went down Bond Street, and home along Oxford Street. The state of the streets was wonderful. All the great ones filled with a motionless mass of carts, waggons, and carriages, and the footways crowded with people. The best illuminations were at Lord Ward's in Park Lane, and at the Turkish embassy in Bryanston Square. In both of them the windows and architectural lines of the building were traced in light, giving the notion of houses made brilliant for a festive occasion. The ordinary devices, such as stars and crowns, have no meaning in them. Seen from a distance across the Park, Lord Ward's house looked like a fairy palace, which, being a well-known and familiar object to all of us, is always selected for comparison. Got home about half-past one, as most people did who were on foot. Carriages did not get home till three or four o'clock in the morning, and the next day not a cab or hired carriage was to be had until late in the afternoon.

*3d June.*—To the Law Institution, Chancery Lane, to preside, as one of the Masters of the Exchequer, at the examination of articled clerks for admission to practice as attorneys. I have been endeavouring to improve the character of the proceedings, and to introduce prizes or certificates of merit for the best candidates. On this occasion the other examiners agreed to have a sort of rehearsal of what an examination conducted with a view to awarding distinctions should be, and marks were given for answers on a rough scheme drawn up by me. Dined at the Law Institution. Thesiger was there, amusing as usual, and I walked away with him.

*25th July* 1856.

DEAR E.—We have had a couple of lectures at Lord Ward's Gallery in the Egyptian Hall on Dante and Alfieri by Signor Arrivabene, who in the first quoted from my translation with great praise. They were *apropos* to the acting of Alfieri by Madame Ristori. We have seen her three times—in Pia, Rosmunda, and Francesca—but unfortunately not in Medea, which is said by most people to be her finest part. She has fine voice, face, and figure, much careful study, etc. etc., and in short has everything but the very highest genius, which leads to total abnegation of self while impersonating a character, and that (real or apparent) forgetfulness of the stage and the audience which constitutes the greatest power of a great actor. Such I have seen in Rachel and Macready, but only in them. We have had one delightful evening with Tennyson, who dined alone with us.

Below is a punning epigram in Latin on the defence of Kars, and its surrender under pressure for food, which may amuse such of your party as may be able to construe it :—

KARS, *September* 1855.

Fama fame ; duo Victores ; nam defuit illic
*Victus:* ibi pariter cuique perennis honos.

I do not know who made it.—Yours affectionately,

W. F. P.

*8th January* 1857.—To private theatricals at Tavistock House. The principal piece was *The Frozen Deep*, written by Wilkie Collins, and in which Edward Pigott, Mark Lemon, Dickens, Augustus Egg (the painter), and the author himself took parts. The two daughters of Dickens and Miss Hogarth, his sister-in-law, were among the ladies who performed. The scenery and act-drop were painted by Stanfield and Telbin, the best artists in that line of the day. All the arrangements were perfect, as was always the case when Dickens managed affairs. Every guest had an assigned place, and the company were summoned from the drawing-room, in which they assembled, to the theatre in the order in which their seats would be most conveniently reached. This was, however, rather an awful affair, and was like the summons from a prison-room in Paris to the guillotine during the Reign of Terror.

*19th January* 1857.

My dear E.—If you are still in want of books for your club, I can recommend to you the *Memoirs of Perthes*, the old German bookseller; but probably your lists are already completed. I have read Guizot's *Life of Peel*, unfortunately in the English, and it is said to be very badly translated.

I am disappointed in it. I don't know why Guizot should be expected to write a good life of Peel, and I don't think he has made the best of it. His authority is Hansard, and no foreigner can understand our ways, so that, with the exception of what relates to the Tahiti difficulty, in which Guizot was himself concerned as the French foreign minister of the day, and which is accordingly treated at disproportionate length, there is nothing of much original value in the book. F—— is to go at Easter to Dr. Huntingford's school at Brook Green, Hammersmith.

We have much enjoyed a New Year's Day dinner at Eastlake's, from which all the guests carried away some little gift, and a day or two afterwards a dinner at Forster's, who, with his wife, now occupies one of the larger houses in Montagu Square. We had Macready to dine with us alone on the 5th, and had a charming evening with him. He is full of education, and has now got at work a school intended to fill up that fatal gap which interrupts teaching in the labouring classes whenever the child's labour begins to be of any profit to the parents. And to effect this he has, at his own expense, opened an evening school at Sherborne, chiefly for the winter months, when there is time left after the day's work is done. In this he teaches himself, and is endeavouring to interest the gentry of the place in it generally.

You may be amused by an anecdote of dress as now worn. Mrs. A—— and her young friend Miss G——, after the experience of the first of Faraday's recent lectures, which were crowded with a large audience, always took off their usual crinolines or hoops, or whatever is their proper name, before they went to the Royal Institution. Think of this—a piece of dress so monstrous that it cannot be worn with comfort in a place where fashionable and full audiences have assembled for the last fifty years. It is a frightful disfigurement, bad enough in the drawing-room, but still worse when used with a walking costume.

*20th February* 1857.

Dear E.—We have lately had Whateley's *Bacon's Essays*, which is, however, hardly a circulating-library book, nor a book to read much in at a sitting. Bacon's very condensed and pithy sentences bear the dilution of W.'s annotations, and the book will be useful as translating into modern habits of thought, and as fortifying by modern instances, the sayings of the old philosopher. I have also read Sir Charles Napier's *Baltic Campaign*—of course a defence of himself at the expense of everybody and everything else.

The night before last I was at Lady Spearman's in Putman Square, and was there in company with Cardinal Wiseman, who had been dining with them. It was strange to see the burly form, the silk robes, the red skull-cap and stockings, quietly moving about in a drawing-room full of ladies and gentlemen, and in nothing but the dress differing from the other guests. He looked to me as if he had just walked off the stage, and yet a living reality of a strange enough kind. No Roman Catholics were present, or one would have seen them go on their knees to his Eminence for his blessing. Just after he was gone in came Mrs. A—— with her young lady, Miss G——, who is a R. C., and was much alarmed and relieved when I told her what must have happened if the Cardinal had been present when she arrived.

*27th February.* — Lecture by Faraday at Royal Institution on the Conservation of

Force, containing some speculations on the nature of gravity, and on the necessity for supposing the existence of a gravitation ether. Prince Albert was in the chair.

The following letter is from myself to Macready, taken in duplicate by a manifold writer sometimes used by me at this date.

*24th April* 1857.

MY DEAR MACREADY—I dined yesterday with Kenneth Macaulay and his wife. He was full of the amusement of his election at Cambridge, and looking forward with delight to being in the House of Commons again, where he had made so good an impression during the short time that he sat for Cambridge before. Thackeray was there. The four Georges have been good friends to him, and many parts of the country remain to be perambulated with them. When he gives only two of the lectures in the same town he receives fifty guineas for each, when all four, thirty or forty guineas. Nearly a guinea a minute this on the highest rate of remuneration. He spoke in some disgust of Mrs. Gaskell's recent *Life of Miss Brontë*, not without personal reason. You should read that book. It is a sad tragedy of ordinary life.

I took F—— to school on Monday, and I have since learned that he was at once put in a high class, and I have every reason to hope that the place will suit him. It is at Brook Green, Hammersmith, and his master is Dr. Huntingford, an Oxford man, and a son, or rather, I suppose, a grandson of the Bishop whose exercises used to engage the attention of youth in my own school days. I had a nice demonstration of filial loyalty from W—— the other day. I was walking with the boys and we met Higgins (Jacob Omnium, you know, and who is at least seven feet high). When we parted from a talk with him, I told them they had just seen the tallest man in London. "No," says W——; "I don't think he is taller than you are, papa!"—Yours truly, W. F. POLLOCK.

*25th April* 1857.

DEAR E.—We of course had passed the name of De Comines in review when we considered the claims of early modern writers to the title of Father of Modern History, and J—— was inclined to suggest him. If the honour was to be awarded for the first time I should rather give it to Machiavelli, and I confess that I was ignorant that in fact the title had been bestowed on any one. It is not alluded to in the life of Philip de Comines either in the *Penny Cyclopædia* or Rose's *Biog. Dict.* I should like to know where it is that Arnold discusses the question.

I shall be very glad to contribute a few books on elementary science to your proposed lending library, and I will look out for the best. I daresay those on the supplemental catalogue of the S.P.G. are good. But what do you mean by the exclusion of works of Fiction? I can well understand that *Little Dorrit*, or the latest novel in three volumes, may not be good reading for the parochialists of Moville; but do you intend to proscribe *Robinson Crusoe* and the *Pilgrim's Progress*, and all the class of excellent and interesting tales, so many of which appear in the aforesaid catalogue of the S.P.G.? Do you wish to exclude all works of imagination in prose and verse? For if you do you are certainly depriving yourselves of the best mode of getting the people to become fond of reading. I know that many very worthy persons have devoted much time, and

I fear not unsuccessfully, in propagating a belief that goodness and stupidity are fast and inseparable allies, and the consequence is that many people who have been plied with dull and dreary tracts, on their first introduction to books in any shape, conceive a total dislike to reading, from which it is difficult ever to recover them. The statistics of the large lending libraries all show that the favourite books are the best works of imagination, and I cannot think that you are doing a politic thing in rejecting them. The R. C. clergy will find no difficulty in prohibiting the reading of the £4 worth of tracts, but I think they would in preventing their flocks from reading De Foe's masterpiece, or other things I could name.

In this year Professor Frankland, F.R.S., at the time Professor of Chemistry in Owen's College, Manchester, favoured us with a course of lectures at the Royal Institution on the Relations of Chemistry to Graphic and Plastic Art, in which I took considerable interest, and I wrote to him with an extract from one of Gilpin's works which I thought germane to his subject. The Royal Academy some time after this date appointed a Professor of Chemistry, but I am not aware that anything has been done towards putting Gilpin's suggestion into a practical shape.

59 MONTAGU SQUARE, *27th April* 1857.

MY DEAR SIR—On the other side I send you the short extract from Gilpin's work which I mentioned to you on

Saturday. He was an amateur artist of creditable ability for the period, and did much to promote a taste for the picturesque. His book appeared in 1786. The Royal Academy, founded in 1768, had then been in the vigorous existence of youth for some years, but neither then nor since has that body—or, as far as I know, any individual painter—done anything towards carrying out the suggestion. The book is the account of a tour in England, the chief part being devoted to the Lakes, and Gilpin and Gray may almost be called the discoverers of their beauties.—I am, yours truly,

W. F. POLLOCK.

E. Frankland, Esq.

"Here (at Nuncham House, Oxfordshire, visited in 1772) are two or three histories by Poussin, which, having turned black with age, leave us to regret that so able a master, though he was never perhaps an excellent colourist, should have been so little acquainted with the nature of colours. The Flemish school, in general, seem to have had the best preparations. But it might yet perhaps be useful in painting, if the nature of pigments could be brought more to a certainty, *and that the painter, like the apothecary, had a sound dispensatory to direct his practice.*"—From *Observations on Picturesque Beauty*, by William Gilpin, Prebendary of Salisbury. 2 vols. 8vo. Lond. 1786. Vol. i. p. 25.

10*th May*.—Dined with Prinseps at Little Holland House, to meet Tennyson, staying in the house, also Holman Hunt, Lord and Lady Goderich, Sir Edward Ryan, Spedding, Coventry Patmore, Mr. and Mrs. Cameron. This was the first of many pleasant visits at the same place, whether to dine or to spend some time in the garden of an afternoon. It was a fine old rambling house, since pulled down, and Watts the painter lived in it, and had his studio there. Many of the rooms were decorated by him. There was a tradition that the duel in which Captain Best shot Lord Camelford in 1804 was fought in a field close to the house, into which the wounded man was carried, and that many years afterwards his pistol-case was found, with one pistol discharged but not cleaned, and the other still loaded. It should always be remembered that Mrs. Prinsep, one of the five remarkable daughters of Mr. Pattle, member of Council in India, was almost the first to discover the genius of Watts, one of the greatest painters England has produced. The beautiful Lady Somers, one of the Pattle family, sat to Watts before her marriage, and it was the exhibition of this portrait which introduced the name of Watts to the general public. Mrs. Prinsep's sense of beauty, and her love for it, gave a charm to her house and all its surroundings. Poets, painters, politicians, writers, and Anglo-Indians of distinction were always to be met there. With all its associations, Little

Holland House was a resort not to be forgotten.

*17th May* 1857.

Dear E.—We performed our christening yesterday at St. Mary's, Bryanston Square. The godfathers, F. D. Maurice and Edward Herries, were present. At luncheon afterwards there was a sponge-cake designed by F——, and surmounted by a wonderful figure of the family crest—a boar, which would have been equally disowned by heralds and zoologists. In its general uncertainty of outline and imbecility of appearance, it rather resembled a conjectural restoration of some extinct animal than anything which roams the woods on the modern surface of the earth; also, base (but substantial) considerations of practical utility had induced the artist to convert the arrow by which the savage beast is transfixed into a means of support, and consequently the arrow stood perpendicular in the centre of the body, with its lower end or point thrust deep into the soil of cake underneath. All this was much admired by a small party of philosophers and artists who dined with us in the evening. Babbage and Professor Frankland of Manchester, who is giving a course at the Royal Institution on the application of Science to Art, Boxall and Oldfield of the British Museum, whom I had asked to meet him, and give him some information connected with their respective pursuits.

*17th June.*—C. C. S. dinner at Star and Garter, Richmond. Spencer Walpole presided.

*15th July.*—Took the boys to see the Tower and the Monument. In the Armoury we heard the remark made by one of the sightseers that the Crusaders were the chaps that fought against Bonaparte at Waterloo.

The following letter was written to my brother, now Sir Richard Pollock, K.S.I.:

TUNBRIDGE WELLS, 23*d August* 1857.

MY DEAR TRIM—I must not attempt to enter on any of the general matters suggested by what has been doing in India. I will only say how thankful we have been and are that your lot has been in the safest part of the country, and how proud that your previous exertions and well-deserved influence with the natives have enabled you to do the good service you have to the State at so critical a time. The news received here yesterday, with the death of Sir H. Lawrence, touched me with an acuter sense of sorrow than all that had preceded it of disaster and horror. For I take it that in a public sense he was about our best man, and I know how well he has always appreciated your merits, and that in him you have lost a good friend and master. Barnard's place, I suppose, may be supplied, but the death of a commander in the midst of active operations must be always more or less of a misfortune.

I trust that when the wreck is cleared away, and the good vessel begins to be got to rights for the future prosperous voyage which I doubt not lies before her, your position will be altered, and for the better. It is impossible to suppose that the absence of so many officers, as heretofore, on civil employment should be recognised as an established element in the order of things when the reconstruction of the Bengal army takes place. Still less can I suppose that in the determination of all such amphibious existences as yours, which I take for granted must be made, you, and such as you, will be remitted back to the discharge of regimental duty. It would be absurd to sequestrate such a man as Edwardes, for instance, from the civil duties in which he has gained such distinction, and in which he has so much experience. The same of yourself and of many others. Yet your places with your regiments must be filled up. My notion, therefore, is that you will be transformed into a pure civilian, in name as well as in fact; and, as you have already won your spurs before Moultan, I fancy you will now give up your red coat without a sigh, and stick to the pen as your chief implement instead of the sword. Tell me how all this is likely to be.—Yours affectionately,

W. F. P.

TUNBRIDGE WELLS, 26*th September* 1857.

MY DEAR E.— . . . We have had Tyndall with us for a Saturday and Sunday. He was fresh from the Glaciers and the top of Mount Blanc, which he had ascended with only one guide, by special permission of the guardians of the mountains, on the ground of his being a working man of science, and not a rich tourist in search of pleasure only. But it is clearly a dangerous proceeding to go so badly attended, and the usual number of guides is as necessary for the safety of the party as it is desirable for their own profit. —Yours affectionately, W. F. P.

TUNBRIDGE WELLS, 19*th October* 1857.

MY DEAR TYNDALL—Thanks for your lines on Richmond and Park. Barring the grander features of mountain and lake, I believe there is as much beautiful country within an hour's reach of London as in any part of England, and perhaps of all that is thus accessible Richmond presents the choicest variety of charming scenery. Since your musings there, although not very many days since, autumn must have made considerable havoc among the foliage. Here the leaves are in a remarkable degree persistent, both in colour and in attachment to their trees, but those on the limes and others of early decadence have already surrendered at discretion, and many a brown and yellow patch on the green of the distant woods, and many a rustling swirl of dry leaves at one's feet, remind one that the year is waning, and help to reconcile us to the coming hibernation in London. We are to leave the sweet nymphs and naiads of these Wells on Friday, and the following day will see me at drudgery again for the old hag Themis.

I thank you for the sight of the volume of Emerson's *Orations*, which I have been reading with interest. It is impossible not to admire that on "Emancipation," and next to it I like "Man the Reformer." There are noble thoughts and fine writing in all of them, but for the most part they seem to me too hazy and indefinite for the highest truth and beauty. They are grandiose and gigantic, but it is size without strength; more like the unsubstantial forms projected on the mist in the Brocken, than like a living Hercules able to kill the real dragons which infest the world. They fail to give me any feeling of effective power, and the same sense of general indistinctness prevents me from recognising in them much of such beauty—of a very high kind—as might exist even in the absence of strength. As to some parts, of which I am bound to say that I do very entirely disapprove, I will not trouble you with any remarks upon them. I will return you the volume from Montagu Square.

Mrs. Pollock sends her kindest regards, and W—— wishes particularly that you should know that he rides without a leading rein, and that he has had two out of the

VOL. II F

three tumbles which are said to be necessary incidents on the road to good horsemanship.

We are going to offer ourselves to dine with the Moores, at Putney Heath, for Wednesday week. Perhaps we may meet then, if not sooner.—Yours ever,

W. F. POLLOCK.

*13th November* 1857.

DEAR E.—We have got Livingston's African book, which is full of interesting matter, but is not very readable much at a time, from the want of skill in the writing—a deficiency which he admits to the fullest extent, and craves the mercy of his readers, saying that he would rather go through Africa a second time than write a book about it again. But the volume furnishes abundance of most important and novel information, and fills one with regard and liking for the devotion, the true charity, the simplicity, and nobility of the man. Wholly free, as it appears, from all prejudices of sect or church, he went about his work in such a spirit as is not, I am afraid, always shown in these enterprises, and claims as his result just so much and no more than has really been for the present effected. You will, of course, see the book before long, so I will say no more about it.

ST. JULIAN'S, SEVENOAKS,
*26th December* 1857.

MY DEAR TYNDALL—You were so kind as to call a few nights since to ask about us. We were out, dining with Forster, and we were sorry to have missed seeing you. *Now I can tell you authentically where we are, and that is*—*here*, a sentence which would be thought full of a deep transcendental meaning if it was found in the writings of a German *metaphysicker*, but which to you, as chiefly a *physicker*, is only intended to mean what it does mean, and from me, as neither, perhaps, if possible, means rather less —the category of place, if you believe in place, that is, and can conceive an absolute *here* more easily than an absolute I. Space being thus disposed of, I may now proceed to that other perplexity, Time, which, whether you may take it to be a function of space, or that of time, in a differential series to be taken as integrated between limits from a central zero to a plus and minus infinity extending both ways, yet does assert itself in gross and palpable forms in clocks, calendars, histories, astronomical cycles, and other tangibilities and substantialities, and cannot wholly be disregarded in these mundane existences of ours, and so tell you that we came here the day before yesterday, and shall remain, as I suppose, until Thursday or Friday next, so that on Saturday we may perchance see you meeting as juveniles round Faraday's Lecture Table. Meanwhile here, and now, we are far more cheerful than I could have expected, and in the midst of a country looking perhaps more green than it should do in Christmas week; the boys well, and enjoying the outdoor and indoor recreations of the place. W—— the other day came to his mother in much indignation at a scientific glossary, in which he had found " Solid, see Fluid," and then turning to the F's, " Fluid, not solid," which, as he justly complained, left him not much wiser than before. Then he framed, quite by himself, his own definition of a fluid as "*stuff that you can't make a hole in*," which is really as good a one as could be given in so few words, as stating one of the most obvious consequences of perfect mobility among the particles. The said W—— sends his love, Mrs. Pollock desires her kindest regards, and I will wish you a merry Christmas and a happy New Year, and so farewell.—Yours truly, W. F. POLLOCK.

# CHAPTER III

### THE COMTE DE PARIS

*7th January* 1858.—I have been at the latter lectures of Faraday's Christmas juvenile course, which has been attended this year by the Prince of Wales and the Orleans young men and boys. At one of them, in describing the terror occasioned by the early use of the electric shock from the Leyden jar, Faraday read the very words of Musshenbroek, its discoverer, who, after taking it once or twice, wrote to a friend, the Abbé Nollet, "that he would not take it again—no, *not for the kingdom of France!*" At this the Count of Paris touched his neighbour on the seat, the Prince of Wales, and looked significantly at him, as much as to say he would do that and a good deal more for the kingdom of France. He looks as if he might do something, and has a resolute and strongly-marked countenance.

59 MONTAGU SQUARE,
*17th March* 1858.

DEAR E.—On Saturday we had a pleasant dinner here with the Dean of Westminster (Trench), his wife, and daughter—a handsome, pleasant girl—and others. It was served, for the first time with us, *à la Russe*, and now I only wonder that we have not done so before. It is the greatest comfort to get rid of the carving on the table for a large party. I have always liked it at other people's houses, but there is still more reason for liking it at one's own.

Mr. Buckle is to lecture at the Royal Institution on Friday. The demand for tickets is without precedent. I read his book in the autumn with much interest. It is now beginning to be found out, for no doubt his conclusions put an end to all moral responsibility.

*19th March.*—Buckle gave his Friday evening lecture, on the influence of women on the progress of knowledge, at the Royal Institution. The place was crammed, and he spoke without notes and in the most fluent manner —a very remarkable discourse, the more wonderful because it was his first appearance as a speaker in public, and his life has been that of a secluded student of books, without the discipline of school or university. But my indignation was roused by hearing him attack the methods of the Inductive Philosophy in the very place where Davy and Faraday had lectured and made their discoveries. I had read and noted up the first volume of the *History of Civilisation* very carefully while at Tunbridge Wells in the previous autumn; and before going to bed I wrote to John Murray, in Albemarle Street, offering an article upon it. After consulting with the editor my proposal was accepted, and the paper appeared in his next quarterly issue for the following July. It appeared that none of the scientific men of established reputation had cared to undertake an exposure of the blunders and fallacies contained in the book, on account of the wide range of subjects covered by it, but I thought I saw my way to a sort of general skirmishing attack of light artillery which would serve the purpose. It was amusing afterwards to hear that Buckle said the review must have been written by a very old man, and probably by a clergyman; and it was generally believed that it was the work of the editor, assisted by a committee of scientific men, who had severally contributed to it. Altogether, I had every reason to be pleased with the success of my article, and with the attention it excited. Afterwards I wrote for the same journal notices of the first volumes of Carlyle's *Frederick the Second*, and of Motley's *History of the Dutch*

*Republic*, the latter of which appeared under the editorship of my old Cambridge friend, William Macpherson. The editor declined to insert a paper of mine on British Novelists, written at his request, which he was good enough to praise on other grounds, because too much space was given to the novels of Richardson and Miss Austen, and because I put Richardson above Fielding, and therein differed from his own opinion and that which he told me had always been maintained in the Review. This paper was at once accepted for *Fraser's Magazine* by John W. Parker, the son of the publisher, who was then editing the magazine, and was my first contribution to it.

*18th April.*—Breakfasted with Milnes. Met Spedding, Monteith, Maine. Lady Theresa Lewis says the Peelites are always putting themselves up to auction and buying themselves in again.

*17th May.*—Dined with Venables at Oxford and Cambridge Club. K. Macaulay, William Vernon Harcourt, Chapman, Priaulx, Cook (editor of *Saturday Review*), Garden, Brookfield, Sir Francis Doyle.

*17th June.*—Dined with J. W. Parker at his

rooms over the publishing shop in the Strand, at which he gives frequent men's dinners. Met Theodore Martin, W. G. Clark, Alfred Tennyson. Brought home proofs of "Hanworth," coming out in *Fraser's Magazine.*

*15th July.*—Was elected a member of the Toxophilite Society on Spedding's proposal. I had previously been shooting in their grounds in the Regent's Park, on his invitation, and with tackle lent by him. I believe that at this time Spedding, with his usual quiet perseverance and tenacity of purpose, in a matter which interested him, saved the Society almost from extinction, as the number of members had fallen very low. He was a constant shooter himself, although he never attained a foremost rank in his scores, and his presence and encouragement were a rallying point of returning prosperity. Most of the new members who joined at this time were his friends, and when the subscriptions were not enough to provide for the rent of the ground and general expenses, he was most generous in the share he took in supplementing them. For many years the Archers' Lodge was a favourite resort in the afternoon of my wife and myself. She also practised shooting, and with so much success that a prize was awarded to her on the first Ladies' Day on which she shot; and she afterwards took prizes at Leamington and at the Grand National Meeting at Bath. Further distinctions were within her reach; but unfortunately she was persuaded by an over-zealous friend to use a bow which was too strong for her, and this, with excessive practice, ruined her shooting. For myself it never became more than a means of pleasant open-air exercise and friendly intercourse. I took it up rather too late in life, and did not at this time know of the defect of astigmatism in my eyesight, which made a correct aim very difficult. When Sir William Bowman afterwards discovered it for me, and prescribed the appropriate glasses, I had almost ceased to frequent the shooting ground. We had very agreeable company there, among whom were Mules, of the Tithe Commission Office, a man of fine character, and a first-rate shot; Wetherell, one of his colleagues; Sir Charles Hamilton, Bolton; and sometimes Ford, the champion, honoured us with his presence. I never watched shooting so good as that of Ford and Mules, and the latter, of whom we saw a good deal, was a thorough gentleman and good fellow. Ford's *Treatise on Archery* is one of the best practical books ever written on any subject, and Ford was himself as excellent as his book. Ford's treatise has been rewritten, with much valuable matter added, by Mr. Butt, for many years secretary to the Toxophilite Society, and published in 1887, with a preface by C. J. Longman, himself an archer of note. A little later on Anthony Froude was a frequent attendant at the ground, as was William Spottiswoode, afterwards President of the Royal Society, and both were good shots. Froude's fondness for archery may be noted in his history of Henry VIII.'s reign, when he treats of the special legislative encouragement then given to it. On fine summer days my wife generally had a tea-table on the grass, to which our friends resorted, and I think that all the members who then used to come to shoot were our friends. To me the means of so easily getting exercise in the open air were worth a great deal as a matter of health; and when I had a new coat made, after I had been shooting for three or four months, my tailor was astonished to find how much my chest had increased in girth. I believe that the arrangement with the Skating Club, by which they contribute to the rent, and enjoy the use of the shooting lawn, flooded with water during the winter months, to become, in time of frost, a skating-rink, has ensured the permanent prosperity of the Toxophilite Society. I took a great interest in assisting to bring this about not long before I ceased to be an active Toxophilite, and was gratified by being made an honorary member. We had among us also Sir Henry Ibbetson-Selwin, who was a fair shot, and Henry Alworth Merewether, the eminent parliamentary counsel, was also one of us, and said one of his best things on the ground. Our youngest son, M——, was often there with us, and when a little boy his pet name was Moss. Merewether heard this and said, "I suppose you call him *Moss* to show your *lichen* for him." Another of his pleasantries was the advice he gave to a disconsolate tourist at a Welsh hotel, who complained that he had only three days in which to see all Wales, and wanted to ascend Snowdon and Cader Idris, and did not see how he could do both. Merewether said to him, "Don't you see how it can be managed? Go up Snowdon and come down Cader Idris." At the Toxophilite ground, soon after I succeeded to the baronetcy, I lost a trifling bet or stake to Merewether, and he said, "Put your bloody hand in your pocket and fork out." Certainly the practice of archery, as I knew it among the Toxophilites, combined healthy exercise and skill together with pleasant intercourse and good fellowship in a very remarkable degree. I must not omit to mention that the honorary secretaries in my time were Strong, Richardson (then in charge of Archbishop Tenison's chapel), and William Butt, and the last in a variety of ways contributed much to the prosperity of the Society, and the interests of archery in general.

*27th July.* — F—— was elected a King's Scholar at Eton, with his name first on the roll. Twelve were elected out of forty-five candidates.

*19th November.*—With Donne to see Phelps in Sir Peter Teazle at Sadler's Wells Theatre. It was a good and solid performance, like all that he did. The character was thoroughly understood by him, and was also well rendered, which was not always the case with Phelps.

He made Sir Peter not too old or too ridiculous, and presented him as a gentleman who had not lost his self-respect, nor the respect of the world, by having made an unwise marriage. It was a very different version of the part from that in which Farren was so popular. Farren's Sir Peter, with all its merits, was too senile, and wanted repose and dignity. I like his son better in it, whom I last saw in the play when given by Mrs. Langtry at the Prince's Theatre in Coventry Street in 1885 or '6, with an excellent cast.

In this year was published *New Friends*, written by my wife for our son W——, as *Julian and his Playfellows* had been for F——.

19*th January* 1859.

DEAR E.—We were all at St. Julian's for a week at Christmas, and, with four fine days out of six, spent a happy time there. One evening we had great success in playing the game of Russian scandal. An anecdote or incident (which should be one not generally known) is written down on paper, and then confidentially communicated to one member of the company, who in the same way repeats to the next, and so on, until by this private course of tradition it reaches the last person, who is then called upon to repeat aloud what he has heard. The paper is then read, and it is curious to note how entirely a story will almost always get altered in its passage through eight or ten people.

I suppose you have not yet read Carlyle's *Frederick the Second*—a wonderful book with all its faults.

Did I tell you that the squaring of words has come up again, and that Babbage has been applying some of his deciphering appliances to the subject with very curious results?

I have offered a large reward to any one who can square *Bishop*. I have done Rector, Curate, and Dean, but the Episcopal bench has resisted my efforts.—Yours affectionately, W. F. P.

On one occasion the anecdote chosen for the game of Russian scandal was a story of Follett and my father coming away from a city dinner and looking for their hats, in which Thesiger was assisting, and, pointing to a hat, said to Follett, "I can't find your Castor, but here is Pollock's (Pollux)." It was duly transmitted until it came to the turn of a lady (it was the Dowager Lady Torrington) to send it onwards. She confessed to the gentleman to whom she had to repeat it that she only remembered it was a story about some hats after dinner. He said I only know of one such story, and it must be that, and he accordingly sent on his anecdote. At last it came out thus: "The Duke of Rutland took Theodore Hook's hat by mistake, and Hook said he was sorry it was not a good one." The point of the second anecdote lay in Hook's saying, " I wish I had as fine a beaver (Belvoir) as your Grace." But this too was lost in transmission.

*14th February.*—Was elected a member of the Athenæum Club.

*24th March.*— Dined at John Murray's. Dr. Cureton, Sir Justin Sheil, Elwin (editor of *Quarterly*), and Layard.

*7th April.*— Dinner at home. Dean of Westminster and Mrs. Trench, Lacaita, John Murrays, etc. In evening Thackeray, Babbage, etc.

*13th April.*—Dine with J. W. Parker. Sir George Cornwall Lewis, Owen, Helps, Lord Bury, etc.

*1st June.*—I won a prize in the Derby lottery at the Oxford and Cambridge Club with Trumpeter, who ran third to Musjid and Ticket-of-Leave. For some time he was the favourite, and I stuck to him, because, by a strange chance for me, I had named him. Martin had been asked to do so, and begged me to help him. Trumpeter's sire was Orlando, and I thought of Scott's

"O! for the voice of that wild horn
On Fontarabian echoes borne,
 Which to King Charles did tell
How Roland brave and Oliviere,
And every paladin and peer,
 At Roncesvalles fell"

in *Rob Roy*, as well as of Dante's

"Non sonò sì terribilmente Orlando,"

and I suggested Trumpeter as the name, which was adopted. My prize just served to recoup me for many unsuccessful entries on similar occasions at the Club and at the robing-room at Westminster, where there used to be Derby lotteries, and the Attorney-General of the day always promised to enter a *nolle prosequi* if any one was informed against for taking part in them.

*18th June.*—C. C. S. dinner at Richmond—Horsman presiding.

*27th June.*—Colin Blackburn appointed a judge in the Queen's Bench. I met him just after he had been with Lord Campbell, and he told me that when he offered him a judgeship he at first declined it, believing that it was the place of a County Court judge that was in question, and with difficulty accepted the fact that he was to fill a vacancy in the Superior

Courts. It turned out an admirable appointment, and Blackburn's subsequent elevation to the post of a Lord Ordinary of Appeal in the House of Lords was no surprise, but gave general satisfaction.

*6th July.*—Dined at Vintners' Hall, at their great annual Kenton festival. It was on this occasion, or at some similar one in another year, that I heard the most successful after-dinner speech ever made. The late Lord Wynford, son of the first peer so long Chief Justice of the Common Pleas, was always the important guest at this dinner. His father, when Serjeant Best, had won a great case when at the bar as counsel for the Vintners' Company, and their gratitude was kept up in the next generation of the family. Before dinner Lord Wynford told me of his difficulty in finding something new to say in the speech which was always expected from him, and begged me for some hints. Of course I replied that he knew the place and its ways far better than I did, and that he had only to trust to the inspiration of the moment and all would be sure to go well. When his time came Lord Wynford went over the usual story of his father's connection with the Company, and its traditional maintenance with himself, and how he used to be brought to dine in their hall when a boy, and he wound up by saying: "As I grew older and was about to enter upon life, my father said to me, 'John, it is now my duty to give you some advice upon your conduct. You will be exposed to many temptations, you will often have to decide on what is right and what is wrong, and to take your course accordingly, and I have only one rule to lay down for you. When you are in doubt what to do, look at the Vintners' Company, do as they do, and you will certainly do right.'" This brought down thunders of applause, and I congratulated Lord Wynford as we were going away upon the immense hit he had made.

*17th August.*—To the Old Bailey, where Smethurst was being tried for the murder of his wife before the Chief Baron. Towards the end of the sitting an incident occurred which strongly illustrated the tendency to laugh which always exists in a court of justice, however solemn and serious the occasion may be. It was a very hot and close day, and my father had made repeated demands for more fresh air to be admitted. At last the sheriffs told him that they had come to the end of their means of ventilation and could do no more. "Then," said my father, "open the windows." "The windows will not open, my lord," said the sheriff. "Then break them," said the judge. Upon which one of the ushers, armed with his long white wand, went into the jury-box and, mounted upon the back of another, began thrashing away at the panes of glass in the large window above the jury-box. Another usher, similarly provided, and leaning as far forward as he could from the gallery, while a second man held him to prevent him from falling over, began to attack the upper part of the window, and the two men belaboured it as if they were beating a walnut tree to bring down the walnuts. The effect was irresistibly droll, and for five minutes every one in court, including the judge and the prisoner at the bar, was convulsed with laughter. At last enough glass was smashed to let in the desired amount of fresh air, gravity was resumed, and the case was proceeded with as if nothing had happened.

*9th January.*—To Lord Macaulay's funeral

in Westminster Abbey. As a spectacle there was nothing striking in it, and the service was less affecting than I have felt it to be in the open air, in churchyard or cemetery, when I have chanced to witness the funeral of a total stranger. Much of the service was chanted, and what was read was well delivered by the Dean. The occasion was interesting and solemn, but the surrounding associations did not seem to be altogether in unison with it. The interior of the Abbey was unchanged, except for the open grave, which, to me, looked almost as much out of place as if it had yawned in the floor of a drawing-room. The music, too, so unusual at a funeral, seemed to belong to the ordinary services of the building. Among the persons assembled to do honour to the great man we had lost from among us were so many friends and acquaintances as to give the occasion almost the air of a social gathering. We were in the Abbey by twelve o'clock; the service began, as arranged, punctually at one; all was over, and we had looked into the grave by two. I knew enough of Macaulay to have personal feelings of admiration and regret to mix with the general sorrow for his death, and the universal recognition of his claim to sepulture among the great writers and jurists of his country. While waiting for admission at the door at Poet's Corner, we had some talk with Charles Austin on the pretensions of several persons then living to burial in the Abbey on their decease. He mentioned John Stuart Mill as the man best entitled to this national honour, but I was not able to agree with him; yet I think that the reputation of Mill stood higher at this time than it did towards the end of his life, or than it has stood since his death.

*11th February.*—Came to dinner with us— Tom Headlams, Eastlakes, Groves, Millais, Edward Romillys, Barlows. Romilly has a characteristic anecdote of Jeremy Bentham. Sir Samuel Romilly once asked Bentham to dinner to meet a common friend (George Wilson) just returned from India. Bentham always hated a third person in company, and wrote in reply, " If nothing to say, why meet? If anything, why Wilson?"

*29th February.*—Dined with Eastlakes, Fitzroy Square. Lord and Lady Robert Cecil, Delane, Malins, Lord Justice Turner.

24*th March.*—At dinner Dean of Westminster and Mrs. Trench, John Murrays, Grant Duffs, Dr. Watson, G. S. Venables.

23*d May.*—Dined with J. W. Parker. Theodore Martin, Boyd (A. K. H. B.), Buckle, Arthur Helps, Canon Robertson, Smiles.

20*th June.*—C. C. S. dinner at Richmond —Sir Arthur Buller in chair.

16*th November.*—Funeral of J. W. Parker at Highgate Cemetery. Trench and Maurice officiated. I in coach with Theodore Martin, Helps, and Froude, who has nursed Parker most tenderly during his last illness. The death of Parker, who was the only son of the founder of a publishing house which had rapidly attained eminence, destroyed all hope of its continuance. The father was too old to attend to the business effectually, there was no other member of the family to take it up, and the concern not long afterwards passed into the hands of Longman & Co., together with the proprietorship of *Fraser's Magazine.* Young Parker was a man of considerable intellect and attainments, and of a most affectionate character. The firm made a mistake, as publishers do, in declining to incur any risk in the publication of Buckle's *History* *of Civilisation*, which they undertook only upon terms of his bearing all expenses, and paying them the usual commission on sales. This turned out fortunately for the author, as the book had a considerable commercial success.

*25th February* 1861.

MY DEAR E.—I have been much interested in reading Olmsted's last book on *The Slave States of America*. It puts the whole thing in a miserable and hopeless light, even worse in its dull uniformity of degradation than the horrors of *Uncle Tom*, heightened by the contrast of some romantic touches of humane masters and happy slaves. The man's reports of what he sees and hears are evidently most truthful. His deductions appear to be sound and free from prejudice. I have also read one of his former volumes on Texas, and there is another on *The Slave States of the Sea-board*, which I mean to read. Lighter and more amusing reading has been furnished by two ladies of the last century, Mrs. Delany and Mrs. Piozzi—the first a very charming person, as one always knew her to be, although her letters, and everything about her, have been given at somewhat excessive length by the editorial affection of her great-niece, the present Lady Llanover. I have nowhere met with better or more pleasing pictures of the society of the days in which Sir Charles Grandison and Mr. Thomas Jones flourished. Mrs. Delany's letters are not very clever, but always readable and charming. There are three fat volumes, and there must be at least as many more to bring her down to the days of George the Third, in which one became first acquainted with her through

Miss Burney's *Diary*. As to Mrs. Piozzi, the more one knows of her the less one likes her.

14*th March.*—Dined Herman Merivales. Met Sir Roderick Murchison, Henry Reeves, William Longmans.

15*th March.*—Dined with Froude, to meet Arthur Helps and Theodore Martin as to management of *Fraser's Magazine* during Froude's absence at Simancas. Helps said that Sir Thomas Phillips of Middlehill, who has a celebrated collection of books and manuscripts, is very reluctant to allow any one to see them. The reason is that J. O. Halliwell, who was admitted to the house to consult the MSS., ran away with his daughter. It was remarked that he had been for spelling MSS. with an I in it.

17*th March.*—Little M—— wanted to know how a tulip could grow from a bulb, and asked, "Where does the flower come from?" I tried to explain how it came up from where it lay undeveloped down in the bulb. He thought for a moment, and then asked, "Papa, was your head ever at your feet?" I repeated this to Owen, who said he was much struck by the physiological truth lurking in the question.

*23d March.*—To see Fechter in *Hamlet* at Princess's Theatre. It was a strange but interesting performance. Coming away, with the recollection of the French remark on the famous charge at Balaclava, I said to Boxall, " C'est magnifique, mais ce n'est, pas la guerre." It was a fine piece of romantic acting, but it was hardly Shakespeare. Many of Fechter's innovations and alterations seemed to have been adopted only for the sake of breaking in upon old traditions, and adding further novelties to the sufficiently startling one of a foreigner appearing in one of the greatest of English plays with the training of the Parisian stage and a strong French accent and method of delivery. There were three acts instead of five, a flaxen head of hair instead of a black one, and continual deviations from the established business of the piece as given in the English theatre. But with all this, Fechter's representation of Hamlet was a fascinating and instructive one, melodramatic and occasionally distorted as it was. He had a touch of genius, and he well understood the exigencies and opportunities of the stage, and carried off his defective pronunciation by his entire absorption in his part.

I must always count him among my noteworthy Hamlets. Charles Kemble was the first, seen at the little theatre at Barnwell, in a long vacation at Cambridge. He failed somewhat in the reflective and passionate passages; but was excellent in the lighter scenes of the play. Macready, although he too was not young enough to look the part perfectly when I saw him in it, combined nearly all the requisites for giving the best effect to the character. He could be passionate, philosophical, tender, generous, gallant, courteous, humorous, and witty. His scholarly education told especially in his favour when sustaining the manifold part of Hamlet, and it was the one which he loved the best. "Beautiful Hamlet! farewell, farewell," was the entry made in his diary after he had played the part for the last time. Irving's Hamlet, too, is a thing to be greatly admired and remembered, and it is the great part in which he is seen to the greatest advantage, and by the frequent performances of which he has, perhaps, most contributed to the higher education of the day, and to familiarising his crowded audiences with the masterpieces of our stage. Except these three, I know no other English Hamlet in my time worth mentioning; but on the French stage, Mounet Sully's impersonation, which I have not myself been fortunate enough to see, has made a great impression by its beauty, grandeur, and intellectual qualities. Nor should Faure's appreciative acting of the part, in addition to his merits as a singer in the opera of Ambroise Thomas, be forgotten. In pure melodrama, such as *Don César de Bazan*, *The Corsican Brothers*, *Ruy Blas*, etc., Fechter was pre-eminently good. His Othello was a failure, but his Iago was not without merit.

*19th April.*—Dined John Murray's. Met Motley and his wife; Gleig, the chaplain-general and military historian and writer; Cureton; W. Macpherson, for some time editor of the *Quarterly*, etc.

*20th April.*—Meeting at Lansdowne House of members of Trinity College to further the proposal of a statue of Lord Macaulay to be placed in the college. The Chief Baron was in the chair.

*15th May.*—Literary Fund dinner at Freemasons' Tavern. The Duc d'Aumale presided, and made an admirable speech in English. I sat with Laurence Oliphant, and was to have proposed the toast of "The Travellers," to which he was to have responded. But it got very late, people began to go away, and after having satisfied each other that neither of us wanted to speak, we went away before our toast was reached. Next day, however, it appeared in the report of the evening's proceedings in the morning papers that Oliphant proposed the health of "The Travellers," and that I, who had hardly been out of England, returned thanks. The reporters had evidently gone away too, *et voilà comme l'on écrit l'histoire.*

23*d May* 1861.

DEAR E.—I will answer your question first. The allusion to a modern instance of remuneration to the family of an assassin—or, rather, would-be assassin—was to the case of Cantillon, the man who wished to assassinate the Duke of Wellington in Paris. Napoleon by his will, executed at St. Helena, left him a legacy in express approbation of his intended murder; and in the payment of the bequests of that will by recent French Governments, the representatives of Cantillon have received the money left to him.

I spent my holiday on Whit-Tuesday in going to see F—— at Eton. I saw his own little room for the first time, and very comfortable it looked, with its small library of prize books. We were joined by a boy who shares a boat with him, and the two gave me a pull up the river, I steering them in a luxurious manner, and enjoying the beauty of the day to the utmost on the water and with their pleasant talk. Then we proceeded to the White Hart to give my rowers some dinner, and then to the Castle to see some of the curiosities of the Queen's library. In going down I had made acquaintance with the librarian, Mr. Woodward, a very agreeable gentleman, which resulted in his asking me to come and see him, and bring the boys, and before we parted we found we had several common friends and acquaintances. The miniature collection was the most interesting thing we saw. It begins with several of Henry the Eighth, and comes down to the Queen's children. A drawer full of young princes and princesses, by Newton and Ross, was most charming. It was like a bed of roses. There are also portraits of historical characters, etc., very many more than we could look at in the time at our disposal. There is a magnificent collection of prints and drawings, filling one room, and forty thousand volumes of books, comprising some typographical rarities. The Prince spends a good deal of time in the library, and it is hard to get him away from it. Message after message comes to him as the dinner hour approaches, and sometimes the last is that "Her Majesty is at table."

EQUITABLE LIFE OFFICE, BLACKFRIARS,<br>
4th September 1861.

My dear Father—I am able to answer your inquiries about the "flint implements" better than I otherwise could have done, by a curious enough series of coincidences. In driving to the station this morning from St. Julian's I met the postman, and got your letter from his bag. In the same carriage with me on the railway was a gentleman just come from abroad. We talked a good deal about France, and iron ships, and so forth, he having been at Cherbourg. At last, and only a few minutes before arriving at London Bridge, he said he had been looking at antiquities at Abbeville. Then I, remembering that many of these flint weapons had been discovered in Normandy, in what geologists call "the drift," asked my new acquaintance if he had seen any of them. He replied by taking a basket from under the seat, which was filled with specimens, although of a ruder kind than the one figured by you. I had now only time to ask him for the name of the best book or writer on the subject, and he put into my hand a paper from the *Transactions* of the Royal Society, by Prestwich, and it was Prestwich himself whom I had been so fortunate as to fall in with. Babbage, of whom in science it may be said, *nihil est quod non tetigit*, etc., has written a beautiful little paper on the subject, but dealing only with the geological part of it. I have always felt much difficulty in recognising all these objects as the results of human art. The evidence is certainly strong from their appearance. It is not easy to suggest how such regular fractures could be produced, except by the application of well-directed blows given with the design of imparting a particular shape. But the very multitude of the flints staggers me. It looks as if all the people could have done nothing else but make them; and I do not believe that any have yet been found associated with other remains or vestiges of human existence. Altogether the considerations suggested by these discoveries are most interesting, and they must be taken as pointing at least to the strong probability of an intelligent race inhabiting the earth long, very long, before the earliest periods hitherto assigned, even by geologists, to the appearance of man upon the face of the globe.—Yours affectionately, W. F. P.

*12th September.*—We left London for Scotland, taking our youngest boy with us, to pay visits to Arthur Malkin at Corryburg, some miles south of Inverness; to the Grant Duffs, at Eden, near Banff; and to see Cowper, a brother director at the Equitable, at Carlton Hall, near Penrith, on our way home. In posting on from Dunkeld, beyond which the railroad did not then go, we changed horses at Blair-Athol, Dalancardoch, Dalwhinnie, Kingussie, and Bridge of Carr. At Kingussie a lady staying in the hotel sent her maid to ask if she might see our boy in her room, and he went to her for a few minutes. He told us that she was in deep mourning, and had asked his name and given him many kisses and caresses. Probably the poor lady had recently lost a child of her own, and it was a touching incident, but remained unexplained.

CORRYBURG, INVERNESS,<br>
*17th September* 1861.

MY DEAR FATHER—We travelled yesterday from Dunkeld through a magnificent country. We had eighty-five miles to post, and I suppose it is the only remaining piece of road of such a length along which the mail still runs behind four horses. I found the cattle good, and also the carriages, which we had to change only three times. Meaning to start at six, and actually starting twenty minutes later, we got here a few minutes after seven. We made a second breakfast at Blair-Athol, and lunched at Kingussie. The day was fine, a great rarity this year, as we hear of six weeks of rain, and the rivers tell the same story. The Tay, the Garry, the Spey, and the Findhorn, now before our windows, are in glorious force, more full of water than for fifteen years. The three first of these were our only companions yesterday, for we saw nothing the whole distance but the mail which met us. The size and space of the scenery through which we passed produce a grand impression, and, as it is the last such drive one is ever likely to have—passing rapidly, with all the luxury of good posting, through a long succession of varied and picturesque country—one is not likely to forget it. The railroad, with all its monotony, is a bad substitute when speed can be sacrificed to enjoyment.

We are here in a simple establishment in a real Highland home. The fuel in the sitting-rooms is wood. Our mutton and grouse are roasted at a peat fire. We know of no civilisation nearer than Inverness, seventeen miles off. I am now going to assist our host in looking after some grouse.—Yours affectionately, W. F. P.

There was an amusing occurrence one day. Malkin's factor came from Argyllshire, where he lived, and dined at the house. He was an extremely zealous elder of the Free Kirk, and was full of the hardship experienced by that religious community in not being then able to procure land for building churches, etc., from the Duke of Argyll. He was delighted to find that I was well acquainted with the history and merits of the Free Kirk movement, and especially with the great Auchterarder case, on the question of patronage, in which my father had been one of the counsel when it was on appeal in the House of Lords. He was still more pleased to find that I entirely agreed with him in believing that the private patronage of church livings was entirely at variance with the spirit of a Presbyterian Church, and that "the harmonious call" to the charge of a parish should be a real power of appointment in the hands of the congregation. Then we went to the question of sites for churches in Argyllshire, and again I sympathised with him, and led him on to say, with much warmth, that, if he were a landowner, it would be against his conscience to deny to any religious body the opportunities of convenient public worship. To which I replied, " Then, if a Roman Catholic congregation were in want of a site for a chapel, under similar circumstances, you would of course be glad to let them have it ?"—" No," said he furiously, and striking his hand on the table, "that I would not. They are idolators." After this he did not seem to like me so much as he did before.

At Eden was told the story of the Scots minister in a church where it was the habit to give out the psalms to be sung line by line from the pulpit, but who on a particular occasion desired to excuse himself from so doing, as his sight was temporarily impaired. So he said:

"My eyes are dim, I cannot see,"

on which the precentor and congregation, taking it for the first line of a psalm or hymn, sang

"My eyes are dim, I cannot see."

The minister, rather disconcerted, and trying to explain, said

"I meant to make apology,"

which was again sung by the congregation. The minister, getting angry, said

"I only said my eyes were dim,"

again taken up and repeated in singing by the congregation. The minister, exasperated, bawled out

"I did *not* mean to give a hymn,"

sung again by the congregation, and so on. There was also mentioned a Scots minister's prayer for the British navy: "Lord, be as a wall of fire round the ships! Be as a great rock in the midst of them! May they be as immovable as iron!" Not long afterwards I found "the great rock in the midst" in the original Joe Miller of 1730, in which a similar story is told, but of an English bishop, which illustrates at once the adaptability and the permanence of jokes. *Cælum non animum mutant.*

From Carlton Hall I went to pay my respects to Lord Brougham at Brougham. I was told that his hours were uncertain, and that his attendance at the family meals was irregular, but that my best chance of seeing him would be to try to fall in with him on his return from service in the family chapel to the house. In this I succeeded, and I think he remembered me; but he seemed very feeble, his face was of ashen gray, and he said only a few words. He looked like a shadow of the past.

11*th December.*—I was appointed a trustee of the Soane Museum in Lincoln's Inn Fields. It came about in this way. Among other curious provisions made by Sir John Soane in bequeathing his house and collections to the nation, it was prescribed that the curator should be an architect who had won a medal at the Royal Academy, and that he should be chosen by that body and presented to the trustees of the museum by the Royal Academy. The Academy very wisely appointed Bonomi, the well-known Egyptologist, who seemed made for the place and the place for him; but the trustees had refused to induct him on the ground that he did not fulfil the condition of being an architect, never having actually practised his profession, or done anything but design a park lodge for a personal friend. Things were at a dead lock; there had been a strong feeling in the matter among the trustees, and one or two of them had resigned. At this juncture Hardwick, the architect, asked me to help him and the others who were in favour of accepting Bonomi's appointment by becoming a trustee, and I consented. The opinion was then taken of Sir Roundell Palmer, who advised that there was no legal definition of the status of an architect, and that Bonomi's professional education and competence to act as such gave him a sufficient qualification for the office of curator. Accordingly he was duly admitted, and the affairs of the trust went on as quietly as ever. The house cannot be altered, and the collections cannot be in any way increased;

all that can be done is to take the best means for their preservation, and the house, if left intact, will some day, although with many peculiar arrangements, be a valuable specimen of a London dwelling-house of the period. The library and art collections are extremely interesting. Among the books are a very fine copy of the *Landino Dante* of 1481, with all the engravings; and copies of the first four folios of Shakespeare, and some finely illuminated MSS. The museum also contains Hogarth's Rake's Progress and Election pictures, a good Turner, and a large Canaletto, with other pictures of mark. In my time as a trustee the most important pictures were put under glass—a sad necessity for works of art in London—and much was done otherwise for the due preservation of the various objects in the museum, including the placing of the great Belzoni sarcophagus in a glass case. It would be wrong to destroy the Museum as it exists by transferring its contents to other public collections, as much of its interest would be destroyed by such a step; and it is now made easily accessible for the public, and is always open to students.

59 Montagu Square, 22*d December* 1861.

My dear E.—I am writing at the close of the saddest day I ever saw in London. The signs of general grief have been everywhere seen and heard; all the public offices have been closed; nearly all shops shut; all faces wear an air of sorrow and concern. The occasion is indeed one to justify every expression of admiration, regret, and sympathy for the Queen and her children; and the general sadness contrasts strangely with the preparations for Christmas festivities, which, however, have been, in consequence, much abridged. Posthumous praise has never been so well deserved as in the case of all the encomiums which have been written on the Prince Consort. He had himself told Dr. Jenner that he knew he would not be appreciated until after his death; and there was truth in this, although for many years past the unreasonable attacks upon him had subsided, and all persons whose opinions were of value had learned to recognise his excellent conduct on all occasions, his great abilities, and his patient devotion to his duties. From the beginning of the illness the physicians thought badly of it, but it was not until the Friday in last week that people in general became anxious. Indeed, except in London circles with some special information, I suppose that the fatal termination must have taken all the world by surprise. Saturday was a time of intense anxiety. I suppose the name was omitted in the prayers in all London churches on the Sunday, and that gave the first information to many. The accounts of the Queen have been good from the beginning. At the end of two days she sent for the Cabinet boxes, and began to read papers and think of public work again. Poor lady! No union in private life was distinguished by more entire confidence, mutual reliance, and affection.—Yours affectionately,       W. F. P.

# CHAPTER IV

### A DOMESTIC PLAY-BILL

*14th January* 1862.—This evening we had a juvenile entertainment at home of two acted charades and a proverb. As our drawing-rooms were not very ample, the play-bill was headed with the line—

" Our room be magnified, but not our faults."—
SHAKESPEARE ;

and I fear a great many worthy persons, among whom was Faraday, spent some time to no purpose in hunting for it in their Shakespeares. This was the time when Fechter was playing Hamlet with many innovations, and the bill contained a notice that the last piece was founded upon an illegible MS. discovered in pulling down the ancient edifice of the drama. " The Management," it went on to state, " desires to show itself sensible of the absurdity and danger of following worm-eaten tradition; but the Play being new, it is difficult on this particular occasion to exhibit the proper amount of contempt for the established customs of the Stage. For the novelty of the Piece excludes the possibility of its beauty having been injured by the representations of a long and illustrious line of great Actors. Wherever it has been possible, however, to cast off the fetters of convention, this has been done; and the Audience will be pleased to accept as a proof of this assertion the varying size of the performers, and especially the fact that the Heroine is a good deal taller than the Hero." M. Prudhon was named in the bill as the property-man. His famous saying, " La propriété c'est le vol," was then being often repeated.

*28th January.*—To Haymarket Theatre to see Sothern as Lord Dundreary in Tom Taylor's piece of *The American Cousin*. The part was made irresistibly droll and quaint by the actor, who indeed had raised it to the place of *premier rôle* from being only a secondary one, to the extent indeed of almost displacing everything else. The piece had an enormous run, and for a long time Sothern appeared in nothing else.

*4th February.*—Drank tea with Faradays at Royal Institution, and played at squails.

*1st March* 1862.

DEAR E.—There have been some interesting lectures at the Royal Institution lately, the most striking of them being one by Huxley on the presumed great antiquity of the human species, which he is inclined to put much further back than has been done by any previous speculations. No moderate extension of the usually received period would satisfy his demands, which rise to the figure of hundreds, or even thousands of thousands of years. Sir Charles Lyell is bringing out a book on the subject, which will no doubt be chosen as a point of assault by those wise religionists who think they can separate creation from the Creator, and who choose to see danger to spiritual belief in every fresh discovery in physical science, and fancy that Truth is not at unity with itself, and that it can be in danger from the varying phases of scientific theories of the material universe.

Lyell's book on the *Antiquity of Man* was published in 1863, and a review of it appeared in *Fraser's Magazine*, for which he was so good as to thank me, saying that it had given him more pleasure and satisfaction than any other notice of the book.

*19th March.*—Dinner at home. Sir Walter James and his daughter, now Mrs. Godley,

Brookfields, John Murrays, Froudes, William Spottiswoodes. Afterwards came in, Moores, Barlows, Dr. Watson, Theodore Martins, Holman Hunt, Woolner, S. Laurence, G. Scharf, F. W. Gibbs, Maurices, Tom Hughes, Herman Merivales, Grant Duffs, and Rawle, a Philadelphian lawyer.

*10th April.*—Dined with Tyndall at Royal Society Club, and with him to Burlington House to hear Warren de la Rue give the Bakerian lecture on the eclipse of 1860.

*14th May.*—Dined Eastlakes. Lord and Lady Cranworth, Lord and Lady Robert Cecil, Lady Essex, etc.

*30th May.*—Sat next to Carlyle at Milnes's round dinner table in Upper Brook Street. Louis Blanc was there, on the other side of the table, whom Carlyle described as a little man looking as neat as if he had just come out of a bandbox, and with no great commendation of his accuracy as an historian. Then he asked if I would like to be introduced to him after dinner. I answered rather emphatically, "No, thank you!" which amused him. Presently afterwards it happened that with the same words I successively declined several dishes and wines that were handed round, and Carlyle remarked, "So it's always 'No, thank you,'" and he got into one of his uncontrollable and boisterous fits of merriment, laughing enormously every time I repeated "No, thank you." I could not help joining in the laugh, until at last Milnes called out to us and wanted to be admitted to share the joke, which of course was impossible with Louis Blanc sitting opposite to us, and so it passed. This was one of the frequent instances of Carlyle's power of enjoying fun, and no one who had often seen him in this mood could bear to see him described as the morose and ill-natured person he was after his death made to appear to have been.

*18th June.*—C. C. S. dinner at Richmond. G. S. Venables presided.

*26th June.*—Came to breakfast at home—Lacaita, Froude, Woolner, Donne, Spedding, young Everett, son of the sometime United States minister in London, and himself now at Cambridge, or just leaving it. Herman Merivale and the Franklins staying with us.

*28th July.*—W—— was elected a King's Scholar at Eton—No. 11 on a chosen list of twenty-one, out of eighty-three candidates.

*1st August.*—We had at breakfast Arthur Stanley, Venables, Lacaita, Boxall, Knight Watson, Spedding, and A. K. H. Boyd, the Country Parson of *Blackwood's Magazine*.

*1st September.*—Went from St. Julian's to lunch with Lord Stanhope at Chevening. He showed me his Pitt relics, and made me very happy by giving me a piece of his writing—notes for a speech on some financial question, made not long before his death. I asked Lord Stanhope what had become of the silver inkstand known to have been given by Pitt, when on his deathbed, to Bishop Tomline. Lord Stanhope said that he had learned its fate from Lord Harrowby (at whose Cabinet dinner the Thistlewood murder plot was to have been executed), who was once dining with a party at the bishop's when some one inquired about the inkstand. The bishop at first put the question by, but was at last compelled to say that he had exchanged it away to his silversmith in part payment for some wine-coolers. Very few relics of Pitt are in existence, and these are at Chevening, or in the possession of Pitt-Taylor, the County Court judge, and author of the work on *Evidence*, who is a descendant of Pitt's father, the great Lord Chatham.

There was a very pleasant time in the autumn of this year spent in the Lake Country. First in a house taken at Grasmere, then on a visit at Greta Bank, Keswick, and another to the James Marshalls at Coniston, and ending with some days at Rigg's Hotel, Windermere, where Crabbe Robinson turned up in wonderful vigour, and talked the whole of one evening to us. He told us that Sara Coleridge said of Wordsworth that he wrote like a poet, of Henry Taylor that he looked like a poet, and of Aubrey de Vere that he lived like a poet.

*9th January* 1863.—Dine with Froude, and with him to Carlyle at Chelsea.

*21st January.*—To visit Mr. Erskine (ex-judge) at Eversley. The following day was Sunday, and Kingsley officiated and preached. It was surprising to find how entirely his usual stutter disappeared when reading the prayers and when in the pulpit.

*28th January.* — To Huxley's lecture at College of Surgeons. There was erected behind him the same series of skeletons which used to appear during the time when Owen was lecturing. A magnificent specimen of *Homo sapiens* stood at one end, and between this and the skeleton of a lemur were various types of apes, anthropoid and otherwise. The two lecturers drew very different conclusions from them. Owen said, Look at that noble and erect form of man and compare it with the monkeys' skeletons passing through a process of degradation down to the wholly grovelling and quadrupedous lemur, and can any connection be sustained between the first and the last? Huxley would say that it was impossible to resist the conclusion that the lowest form had gradually been developed into the highest. I sat sometimes by Bishop Wilberforce at Owen's lectures; my companion at Huxley's was Bishop Colenso.

10*th March.*—Prince of Wales's wedding. In the evening I went out with Tyndall to see the illuminations. In Pall Mall, at the bottom of the Haymarket, the crowd and crushing were frightful. We were for some time jammed against the lamp-post in the middle of the roadway, without being able to move, and sustaining a severe pressure. It must have been very bad and dangerous for people not as tall and strong as we were. I had not been in such a scene since the Queen's wedding-day, when a dinner in celebration of the event was given in the Hall of the Inner Temple, after which I went out with Kenneth Macaulay. In front of Northumberland House two opposing torrents of people met, and there was a surging vortex of struggling humanity, in which Kenneth was helplessly torn away from me. The next moment a young man of short stature begged me to assist him in protecting his sisters from the crowd, and I had only time to say I would do what I could when another violent rush separated us, and I found myself with the distressed damsel on my hands. I got her out of the thick of the people as soon as possible, and we took refuge under the statue of Charles I., where it seemed likely the brother might come to look for her. Here we waited some time, until my charge said she thought she had better go home. Home might have been Clapham, or Bow, or some distant suburb, and I was glad to find it was no farther than over Blackfriar's Bridge. So we walked quietly in that direction along the Strand, till we got as far as Somerset House. Then there were cries of "Oh, John!" and "Oh, Jemima!" The damsel flew to her brother, who had been taking home the other sister, and was now going in search of the lost one; the two disappeared, without a word of thanks, and I went on my way rejoicing at being safely relieved of my responsibility.

16*th May*.—To see Macready at Cheltenham. There was a discussion on the words "he has no children," spoken by Macduff in the play of *Macbeth*. Do they mean that Macbeth has no children, and therefore no revenge against him can be equal to the suffering he has inflicted upon me (Macduff) by destroying mine? Or, that he (Malcolm) has none, and therefore cannot understand my loss, and the insufficiency of any revenge for it? Or, is it spoken by Macduff of himself, dwelling, in abstraction, upon his own desolation, and not heeding what is said to him? Macready preferred the last suggestion, as being capable of the most effect on the stage, and as conveying the most pathetic signification. But is there another instance in Shakespeare of such a use of the third person for the first?

23*d May*.—To Max Müller's last morning lecture at the Royal Institution, and afterwards with him and the two Tylors to see Christie's collection of anthropological antiquities, in Victoria Street. He spoke of modern mythology as seen in the changes in the names of signs of taverns. "The Plume of Feathers" becoming "The Plum and Feathers;" "George Canning" turned to "George and Cannon," but for this he could give no authority; Brazen-nose from Brassinarium, the brewery upon the old site of which the college stands. There was some talk on the difficulty of tracing the origin of a lie. Sometimes rationalism itself has its mythology. The common story to explain the eleven thousand virgins of Cologne is that there was a virgin called "Undecimilla," but nothing is forthcoming to show that there ever was a person so called. Max Müller was for deriving *barnacle*-goose from Hi-bernicula, the goose having come from Ireland; but there is no evidence of this. The resemblance of the Lepas to a bird with feathers is enough to account for the popular belief that the goose came from the barnacle.

*1st July.*—To see *Romeo and Juliet* at Princess's Theatre. A young French actress, Stella Colas, was the Juliet—very pretty, clever, and charming. She played the part so well and looked it so admirably that her strong foreign accent was forgotten, and it was one of the best impersonations of the part I have seen. It had the *abandon* of the South, which it is so difficult for a Northern European or American to assume, and there was the youth and the beauty, which also cannot be artificially created, but must naturally exist.

*15th August.* — Dined with my brother Charles, at Putney, and met Mr. and Mrs. Goldschmidt (*née* Jenny Lind), who were then his neighbours. I was next her at dinner, and happened to mention my love and admiration of Sir Walter Scott's novels. She said she could not abide them. I ventured to ask if she had read them, and she said, "Yes; but they do my soul no good," and turned her back on me for a short time, but soon made it up again. She had a soul indeed, whether improved or not by Walter Scott, when one saw the acting and heard the singing, which touched one to the heart.

Freshwater, Isle of Wight,<br>
16th October 1863.

Dear E.—We remain here until Tuesday, when we go to town for a couple of days, then to pay a four days' visit in Sussex, and afterwards settle at home for the winter. We have found Freshwater very agreeable. For society we have had the Tennysons, the Franklins (he, the Colonel, commanding the Artillery in the island; she, the Lucy Haywood of Liverpool in former times, to whose father's hospitalities and kindness we owe so much), and Mrs. Cameron (wife of the legislative member of Council at Calcutta, who succeeded Macaulay in that office), who has been as kind and amusing to us as she is to all who have the advantage of her friendship. There have also been visitors to ourselves. We have had Tyndall, George, and Donne, the last of whom only left us to-day. The weather was stormy at first, and we are ending rather wildly, but, on the whole, we have not had any serious inconvenience or hindrance from it.

I am glad that one of the family at least felt the earthquake, which did not affect this peaceful island, and F—— is to be congratulated on being the person to enjoy that honour.—Yours affectionately,  W. F. P.

The geology at Freshwater is very interesting, and the natural arrangements are like a museum on a large scale, as there is so much to be seen within a small compass, and it is all so accessible. There are places where you can get fossils out of the ground as easily as you could take them from the drawers of a cabinet. Thirty years ago this would have made me supremely happy, and I find it still very enjoyable.

At Freshwater we occupied the best part of a farmhouse called Easton, with a good garden, and all the attributes of a gentleman's house, which was a charming residence; and I made several geological excursions with Keeping, a most intelligent practical man, who collected fossils and acted as guide. He was afterwards an assistant in the Geological Museum at Cambridge, under Sedgwick, and was employed by John Evans to go to Abbeville and watch the finds of flint implements there. As he had been a working quarryman, and did not know a word of French, his presence gave complete protection against all fraud and collusion.

*12th November.* — Edward Romilly told me an anecdote concerning Napoleon III. He was at Geneva with his mother a year or two before the affair at Strasburg. They were at the house of Mr. Haldemand (Romilly's uncle), and Hortense complained to him of her son's want of ambition. "Vous voyez, il n'a pas un grain d'ambition. Le voilà qui dessine votre fontaine" (he was drawing at the time). "C'est la simplicité même."

59 MONTAGU SQUARE,
*20th November* 1863.

MY DEAR E.—Trench's friends are as pleased as they can be by his elevation to the archbishopric, involving as it must his removal from London, and I think Ireland is much to be congratulated on the acquisition of such a man. The rumours that Stanley was to be appointed seem to have served as a *paratonnerre* to carry off some indignation that might otherwise have been stronger against him, and he appears to be accepted by all parties with something like satisfaction. Counting him as an Irishman, he is said to be only the fourth appointed to an Irish archbishopric since the Reformation. The other Primate (a Beresford) was the third, and the last Primate, Whateley, the second. Who the first may have been I know not.

Have you yet seen Froude's two new volumes, beginning the reign of Elizabeth? I am just finishing them. They are intensely interesting. The story of the end of the wretched Darnley is admirably told. Occasionally the reader may feel rather smothered in the dust of Simancas; but the temptation to make a large use of such a mine of unexplored materials must have been strong. The review of it by Milman in the *Quarterly* is good.—Yours affectionately, W. F. P.

*12th January* 1864.—Acted proverbs at 59 Montagu Square, in which the whole family appeared. F—— and W——, both now at Trinity, under the names of Mr. Newcourt and Mr. Trincolocamby.

*11th February.*—At dinner Alfred Tennyson, Spedding, Tyndall, William Herschell.

*17th February.*—Dined with Woolner, with whom Tennyson usually stayed at this time when in London. Met him, Spedding, F. Palgrave (with whom Tennyson used to stay). A. T. read to us "The Aylmers," and "The Lincolnshire Farmer," the names of which were not then definitely fixed.

*23d February.*—Dined with Theodore Martins. Froude, Venables, Millais, Robert Bell, Miss Jewsbury, Helps, Flower (the Mayor of Stratford-on-Avon).

*10th March.*—Dined with Alfred Tylor at Stoke Newington, and went there with Emerson Tennent. On the walls of the rooms there were water-colour drawings by the Queen's daughters, and on the drawing-table (but not displayed for show) was an album with children's letters from them and their brothers to the Tylor family. I asked about it, and was told that Tylor had married a daughter or niece of Mr. Allen, the well-known scientific and manufacturing chemist of Plough Court, and that his wife had inherited from him a friendship with the Royal Family commenced between the Duke of Kent and Mr. Allen, who was one of the Duke's executors, and had a principal share in the management of his money matters. This friendship had been always kept up, and the births and marriages in the Royal Family were always announced to the Tylors. When the Princess-Royal came over to England with her children, Tylor and his people were summoned to see them at Windsor, and all the usual incidents took place of an old family connection. The Queen never forgets friends, nor any duty of any kind.

*5th April.*—To Drury Lane with Tyndall to see Phelps in Falstaff. Like every part undertaken by him, it was thoroughly well understood, but he could not give expression to his intentions. Instead of the unction required for the fat knight, all was as dry as "the remainder biscuit after a voyage," and the performance left one in a state of admiring and regretful dissatisfaction at its failure.

59 MONTAGU SQUARE,<br>
10th *May* 1864.

MY DEAR FATHER—I have sent to the Court of Exchequer the two last published volumes of Clark's *Shakespeare*, which he gave to me at Cambridge on Saturday for transmission to you. We went to Cambridge to see F——, and found him very well and happy. He has pleasant rooms in the New Court, looking out over the gardens of

Trinity Hall. Among his books are conspicuous your *Thucydides* and *Tacitus* prize books, rejuvenescent in fresh backs, and ready to welcome their successors. We dined with Thompson (Greek professor) on Saturday, where we met Adams the astronomer and others of less note. On Sunday we breakfasted with F., and were much pleased with his most intimate friends, who came to meet us. We heard the Bishop of Oxford preach after evening service at St. Mary's. It was a frightful sermon. He is engaged in a crusade to uphold the dogma of everlasting damnation in spite of the Privy Council. According to this Christian divine, the tenet in question is the choicest morsel of comfort in all religion; to doubt it is, to question the goodness and love of God in the tenderest point. It is the foundation of all hope, the corner-stone of charity.

The face that one associates with courteous smiles and polished talk was deformed by fury. Hatred of his theological opponents glared from his eyes. His plump fingers seemed to be clawing at them. His whole appearance was transfigured to what one may conceive as that of an old Dominican preaching the faith of the Holy Office.

"Humanity craved for it; the expectation of endless torment was always planted in the breasts of men. Even heathen antiquity required it. It was the one sound point in Paganism."

As I listened, my eyes fell on the usual letters embroidered on the pulpit-cloth—the I.H.S.—and I thought they can mean no longer "Jesus Hominum Salvator," but must be taken to stand for something else, which I will suggest to you when we next meet, they seemed so little to accord with what was being delivered from the interior of the pulpit.

The judgment of the Privy Council has done much, but

the spiritual liberties of England may not yet be quite out of danger. I don't think the sermon was much liked by the congregation, and the Bishop would hardly have dared to preach it to the University congregation at the same place in the morning.

I met the Bishop two or three days afterwards in London. He said, "I saw you among my supporters at Cambridge on Sunday." I ventured to reply, "I am always glad of an opportunity of hearing your Lordship preach, but you must not count me among your supporters on this occasion." He rejoined, with his usual urbanity, "I know it well; I was watching your face all the time."—Yours affectionately,
W. F. P.

*18th May.*—Literary Fund Dinner at St. James's Hall—the Prince of Wales in the chair. It was the first time that H.R.H. had ever presided at a public dinner, and he acquitted himself with great ability and success. The large hall was crowded with diners, and the galleries were full of ladies. The list of donations was, as might have been expected, an unusually long one. As one of the treasurers of the Fund, it fell to my lot to read it out after dinner, and I was not sorry to be interrupted by a message from the Prince to the effect that enough had been given out, and that the remainder need not be proclaimed. The Prince's success as president on this occasion was largely due to the pains and trouble previously taken by him to qualify himself to fill the post well, and it was the commencement of a long series of similar duties discharged by him in a true spirit of benevolence and devotion to the obligations of his station.

*1st June.*—C. C. S. dinner at Richmond—Charles Merivale in the chair.

*2d June* 1864.

My dear E.—We had a good sight of the Volunteer Review in Hyde Park on Saturday, sitting in the second row of spectators in the reserved seats, and at no great distance from the place occupied by the Prince and Princess. The best feature in the day's show was the large force of artillery who marched past, 2000 strong, of various corps. Colonel Creed commands one of the London battalions, which is said to be the best, and his heavy guns looked formidable enough as they rolled along. We thought the Cambridge University Corps the best looking on the ground. F—— was with it, but we could not recognise him in the mass as they went by. We go on Saturday (to stay till Monday) to Kitlands, which ought to be in great beauty now, and I hope the severity of the weather will have abated somewhat by that time. One may like London, and yet be glad to escape for a little into the pure green at this season.

*4th June.*—Came to breakfast, Lord Houghton, Venables, Spedding, Cowell, Charles Merivale ; and a fortnight afterwards came Sir

Walter James, Froude, Aubrey de Vere, and Mr. John Walter.

*19th June.*—Breakfasted with Woolner, to meet Alfred Tennyson and Spedding.

*29th June.*—Met Herbert Spencer, Spedding, R. Browning, G. H. Lewes, and Holman Hunt at breakfast at Houghton's.

*13th August.*—Evening with Carlyle at Chelsea. He said his wife had read through Browning's poem of *Sordello* without being able to make out whether Sordello was a man, or a city, or a book.

It was during the autumn visit at St. Julian's in this year that my son W——, at home for the Eton holidays, was reading the *Ars Poetica* of Horace with me, in an edition with the notes of Bond. One day he construed " Hic meret æra liber Sosiis," " This book will gain money at Sosii." I asked what he understood by "Sosii." He replied, " It was a city famous for books;" and on my surprise at this, he said, with an air of authority, " It is so in the notes." I looked to the bottom of the page, found the short note " Sosiis, *bibliopolis*," and saw how he had been misled. Βιβλιόπολις would indeed be a very good word, if it had ever existed.

*27th August.*—Spent day at Canterbury from St. Julian's, with Canon Robertson. A considerable work of restoration of the masonry of the Cathedral was going on, and Robertson told me that the soundest old stones were always found covered with moss. This would make a fine Conservative illustration.

EASTON FARM, FRESHWATER,<br>ISLE OF WIGHT, 12*th October* 1864.

MY DEAR E.—Your last letter was very near reaching me in Ireland, where I have been away from this place on a short trip. I found my old recollections of Dublin many years ago were very indistinct. The first sight of the streets is disappointing, but the buildings and many of the street-landscapes are fine, and it improves on acquaintance. Of the inhabitants I saw little, but intended hospitalities were rising in various directions, by which I should have been glad to profit if there had been time. I was lucky in finding the Archbishop when I called at his town house in Stephen's Green, which is in the hands of workmen, but was unable to dine with him, as he asked me to do at Bray, where he is now living. The travelling *via* Holyhead is certainly magnificent. In going I dined at the Athenæum at 7, left Euston Station at 8.45 P.M., and was seated at breakfast in Dublin at 9 A.M., after a leisurely toilet. So in coming back, I had an early breakfast in Dublin, and dined at the usual time at the Euston Hotel. The time at Freshwater has been pleasantly filled. We see a good deal of Mrs. Cameron, the presiding genius of the place, and also of the Tennysons; and there are always interesting people coming and going. Henry Taylor (*Philip van Artevelde*) was here during my absence, I only seeing him arrive, and spending his last evening in company with him, but J―― saw much of him. Yesterday I took Anthony Trollope a walk to the Needles, and he is coming to us this evening. While the boys were with us we had readings of Shakespeare's plays, which were thought successful, and gave great delight to our agricultural hosts. The walks about us are neverending in beauty and variety, and we have croquet on our lawn for more indolent exercise. By the bye, I played part of a game at the Under-Secretary's Lodge in the Phœnix Park, and noted a diversity of manners and customs, as illustrated by the different way of placing the hoops, and by their having three sticks or goals instead of two, which must make the game interminable. I saw most of the numbers of the *Owl*. It had clever things in it, but was light and flimsy—a sort of *Punch* for the upper classes of London society. Punch made, as it were, with noyeau instead of vulgar rum, and acidified with selected superfine lemons, sweetened with the choicest crystals of sugar-candy, and mixed with some less common element than water, but less racy and potent than the ordinary mixture. It had a great success, and sold well, although the price was 6d. for four pages. Among the best things in it were some imaginary despatches by Lord Russell, attributed to O――. These involved no actual breach of official confidence, for he can have known nothing officially, and nothing was revealed in them; but he ought not to have written them (if they were his), any more than he should have written the papers in *Blackwood* and elsewhere which have procured his exclusion from ministerial circles. He was too abrupt in his passage from the service of the Government to that of the public as a magazine and newspaper writer, and ought not to have written as he did of his late employers. There is a respect and a reticence which ought to survive, at least for some time, the period of actual relationship between master and servant.

I hope Tyndall may come down to us for Saturday and Sunday next; but he is busy, and may not be able to do so.

*22d October.*—Evening at Ffaringford. Tennyson read "Boadicea" and "The Lincolnshire Farmer." The latter gains immensely by his giving the words their proper accent, and by the enormous sense of humour thrown into it by his voice and manner in reading it. I asked Tennyson which he preferred of the two poems, "Enoch Arden" and "Aylmer's Field." He replied "Enoch Arden," which he thought was very perfect, and a beautiful story. "Aylmer's Field" had given him more trouble than anything he ever did. At one time he had to put it aside altogether for six months, the story was so intractable, and it was so difficult to deal with modern manners and conversation. The Indian relative was introduced solely for the sake of the dagger, which was to be the instrument of the lover's suicide.

*2d November.*—Tyndall showed me, in the laboratory of the Royal Institution, the combustion of paper, deflagration of zinc, and heating of platinum to redness by obscure rays passing through iodine dissolved in sulphide of carbon, and opaque to light—a very notable experiment.

*15th November* 1864.

DEAR E.—Müller's trial at the Old Bailey, and the dinner given in the Middle Temple Hall to M. Berryer by the English Bar, have been the chief matters of general interest in which I have had any concern, and both are now rapidly retreating into the past. I do not suppose that my father ever appeared on a public occasion to greater advantage than at the late trial. This is the general opinion. His summing up was a perfect masterpiece, and I regret that I did not hear it given in Court. I was present during the first two days of the trial, but could not afford to give a third day to it, and indeed the interest in the case had quite ceased, so far as it depended upon any doubt of the prisoner's guilt after the speech for the defence had been made.

The bar dinner to Berryer was a great success, but I fancy he does not deserve quite so high a place as an advocate as the complimentary speeches of the occasion gave him. His greatness was rather as a parliamentary speaker than at the bar. But all honour is due to him as a lingering remnant of free institutions in France, and I was very glad to have been able to join in this tribute of respect.

It was at the dinner given to Berryer that Cockburn, then Chief Justice of England, with great eloquence attacked and destroyed the pernicious doctrine asserted by Brougham in the heat of advocacy, on the trial of Queen Caroline, that a counsel was bound to forget everything except the interests of his client, and he used the fine expression that an advocate should wield the sword of a soldier and not the dagger of an assassin. Brougham's saying had not previously been publicly repudiated, either from the bench or at the bar, and it had almost passed into oblivion, but the time for giving it this *coup de grace* was not gracefully chosen, seeing that Brougham himself was present at the dinner, and, owing to the nature of the occasion, no less than to his own age and infirmities, had to endure in passive silence the punishment inflicted upon him by one so much his junior. On returning to town at the end of October from Freshwater, and on my first appearance at the Athenæum Club, I fell in with Tyndall and Huxley in the hall, and was told by them that they were making arrangements for the purchase of the *Reader* weekly journal, and they wanted me to give some literary help. Their object was to provide a better record than then existed of the progress of science, and of the labours and opinions of scientific men, with reports of the proceedings of scientific institutions, and space for correspondence. A limited company was formed to become the proprietary of the paper, and its affairs were to be managed by a joint committee of editors and business men. I promised such assistance as I could give, and as we had to take over the paper rather suddenly, I found I had, with little time for consideration, to undertake the duties of literary editor, but with the very able and experienced assistance of Macdonnell, who was already acting as sub-editor. Tyndall and Huxley were to be the scientific editors, with Lockyer to assist them, and as much help from William Spottiswoode as other work allowed him to give; but I do not remember that Tyndall ever attended at the office of the paper. This was very conveniently situated in Tavistock Street, Covent Garden; and during the brief time of our connection with the paper I used to attend there, late in the afternoon, twice or thrice a week. We had a good business manager in one of the Bohns, and the paper was well supplied with publishers' and other advertisements. F. Galton looked after the geography and travels, and Professor Cairnes undertook the political economy. Llewellyn Davies was already established as reviewer of theological works. We found that the paper had been over-printed, and that there had been a large distribution of gratis copies. This was stopped, and I am sorry to say that no gratitude for past benefits was shown by any of the favoured recipients, not one of whom became a subscriber. Considerable reductions were effected in the cost of printing and other expenses connected with the production of the paper, but the other avocations of our business men did not allow of their giving as much attention to the concern as would have been desirable. We had promises of support from many people of mark. Tom Hughes and J. M. Ludlow had been part proprietors of the *Reader* in its previous stage. Sir Theodore Martin, Aubrey de Vere, Sir Joseph Napier, Donne, Grant Duff, Kinglake, Charles Merivale, Tom Taylor, Francis Garden, W. G. Clark, Aldis Wright, Edward and Albert Dicey, John Ball, J. S. Mill, Watkiss Lloyd, Robert Bell, and others, were anxious to support us, and some of them actually contributed to the paper and took shares in it. Houghton would not join;

he said in a letter to me that he had no money, and did not see the want of a new periodical of the kind, and feared that the existence of a large proprietary would ensure all kinds of discontents and differences. But he added that, although he had written little since his last illness, he would offer something for acceptance if he had any energy left. The first number under the new management appeared on Saturday, 10th December 1864, and we went on for three or four months. It then plainly appeared that without putting in more capital the paper would not become a pecuniary success, and it was disposed of, shortly to terminate its existence by a suicidal act on the part of its new proprietor, who allowed an article to be printed, the writer of which showed that he was not aware of the authorship of Dr. Johnson's famous preface to his *Dictionary*. We had one general meeting of proprietors, as I remember, at which complaint was made of the space allotted to literary matter in the paper, and it was John Stuart Mill who stood forward in defence of the literary editor, and pointed out that this was what really interested the greatest number of readers, and tended most to promote the sale of the paper. It was a curious and unexpected experience for me to find myself suddenly editing the department of *Belles lettres* in a weekly paper, and taking part behind the scenes of literary journalism. I declined to receive any salary, and was in the same boat with my friends as to taking and losing by a share in the adventure. But I had some amusement out of it, and after I got used to the enormous weekly contingent of new publications sent in for notice, became interested in their due allotment to various hands. Our prospectus had stated that every work of note should be reviewed on its own merits, and that equal favour would be shown to all, without considering through what channel they might come before the public. After this announcement it was diverting to have the manager coming to me one day with the proof in his hand of a review which I had marked for insertion in the next issue, and saying, " Please, sir, don't let this go in—at least not now. The book is published by Messrs. ——, and we have two pages of advertisements from them this week. It would do us harm with them." Another time I had sent me a very gushing notice of a child's book, written by a contributor who knew the author, and beginning with "We do not usually notice books of this description, but the unusual merit," etc. Again came in the manager to remind me that for the last three or four weeks, as it was Christmas time, there had been two or three pages of notices of children's books, and begging me to modify the little review of the book in question. This was easily done, Mr. Bohn was made happy, and so I hope were the author and the friendly critic.

*21st November.*—Dined Edward Romilly's. Dean Milman told a story of an Irish lady at the theatre when Mrs. Siddons was acting in *The Grecian Daughter.* She was so much affected as to attract notice, and a gentleman said to her, "It is fortunate Mrs. Siddons is not performing as Isabella, for if this moves you so much, you would hardly be able to support that at all." "What!" replied the lady, "is she not Isabella? I thought she was, or I never would have cried so much at it."

*16th January* 1865.—Came to dine T. Hughes, W. Spottiswoode, Tyndall, Huxley, F. Galton, James Spicer, Burges. This was a *Reader* dinner.

*14th February.*—The following Valentine appeared in the issue of the *Reader* for this week :—

### THE ICE FLOWER
#### TO
#### PR–F–SS–R T–ND–LL.

*14th February* 1865.

Within the ice,
In strange device,
A sleeping beauty, I
 Thy coming wait,
 At happy date,
To bring my destiny.

When through my frame
The electric flame
Its radiant pulses sends,
 I rise from death ;
 Thy fervent breath
My glacial fetters rends.

To nature's lock
Which guards the block
Of ice, thy key applied,
 My soul sets free,
 Which turns to thee
In passion's melting tide.

I pant for you
At thirty-two
By *Fahrenheit* displayed ;
 Or, should prevail
 Another scale,
At zero, *Centigrade*.

# A VALENTINE

In pretty strife,
To start to life
My waking atoms stir;
Their motions fine
To thee incline,
My heart's thermometer.

Folded in frost,
In ice-depths lost,
I droop in cheerless night;
Under thy glow
My petals blow,
Ecstatic with delight.

No heavenly star
That shines afar
With my six rays can vie;
The hexagon
Which you have won
Transcends geometry.

Imprisoned here,
With frozen tear
I weep my frigid fate:
Dissolved by you,
In raptures new
May I ne'er regelate.

Then come, my love,
You powers prove,
Let all your radiance shine;
For evermore
On alp and shore,
I'll be your Valentine.

NOTE.—When the rays from an electric lamp are made to pass through ice—" the ice appears to resolve itself into stars, each one possessing six rays, each one resembling a beautiful flower of six petals."—*Heat considered as a Mode of Motion, by John Tyndall, F.R.S.*

*20th March.*—Dined Houghton's. Met Sir John Simeon, Stirling of Keir, Lord Crewe, F. Locker, Planché, Thom.

*6th May.*—At dinner Mrs. Cameron, Chief Baron, Dr. De Mussy, Spedding. My father told the story of the bet won from Campbell the poet by Lord Nugent, which he had heard from the winner himself. In a company where both were, the talk turned on lines of poetry consisting only of words of one syllable, and some one expressed a doubt whether two such lines were to be found together anywhere. Lord Nugent at once quoted—

> "By that dread name we wave the sword on high,
> And swear for her to live—with her to die."

Campbell said he did not believe in the lines, and asked where they came from. Lord Nugent said, "From your 'Pleasures of Hope.'"—"How do you know that?" replied the poet. "I know it all by heart," said Nugent. "I'll bet you a guinea you can't repeat it," said Campbell. "Done," said Nugent, and the two retired into a window to decide the bet. After a little

Campbell got tired, and said, "I give up; I see you know the poem; don't go any further."—"I will win my bet fairly," said the other, "and must go on unless you double the bet," upon which Campbell pulled out his purse and paid two guineas to the peer who knew his own poetry so much better than he did himself.

*13th May.*—To Cambridge with Tyndall; to Red Lion; dined with F—— in his rooms.

*14th May.*—To College Chapel, and heard Whewell from his stall as Master preach what was in effect a funeral sermon on his wife, Lady Affleck. It was the most painful scene I ever witnessed. Whewell had nerved himself for the effort, and completed his discourse without breaking down. But it was with the utmost difficulty that others contrived not to give way to their feelings of sympathy with him, and there was a strong feeling of relief when all was over. It was a terrible duty for a man to have imposed upon himself. Dined in hall, and afterwards to Thompson's rooms, where was Sedgwick.

*15th May.*—To Senate House with Tyndall, and assisted him in arranging for the experiments to be shown in the Rede Lecture on Radiant Heat.

*7th June.*—C. C. S. dinner at Richmond—Montagu Butler presided.

*21st June.*—To *Twelfth Night* at Olympic. Kate Terry was charming in the double parts of Sebastian and Viola. Certainly one of our most accomplished actresses, with true poetry in her and real devotion to her art.

*22d June.*—My wife gave a prize, a moderator lamp in a Greek vase, to be shot for at the Toxophilite Ground. It was won by Arthur Malkin.

*24th June.*—Breakfasted with me, F. D. Maurice, E. Twistleton, Lacaita, S. Laurence.

*22d July.*—To William Longmans, Ashlyns, Berkhampstead. In the house Froude and his wife, Herman Merivale, and Mr. Doyle, the artist of the H.B. caricatures, the authorship of which was for so long a secret. I made some allusion to them, but Doyle was impenetrable, and plainly indicated his desire not to speak of them.

In the autumn we spent some pleasant days with the Edward Romillys, at their beautiful place of Porthkerry on the Bristol Channel, and were afterwards at Rydal Lodge, taken by us for some time, and paid visits to the James Marshalls at Coniston, and the Speddings at Greta Bank.

20*th November.*—Settled stamps for payment of Court and Office fees at request of Treasury with Master Hodgson for the Queen's Bench, and Master Benett for Common Pleas.

24*th November.*—The Carlyles dined with us. Tyndall, De Mussy, Mrs. Cameron to meet them.

18*th December.*—At dinner Anthony Trollopes, Alfred Thesigers, Matthew Arnolds, Miss Wynn.

# CHAPTER V

## THE BREAKFAST CLUB

19*th January* 1866.—Tyndall lectured at R. I. on Radiation of Heat, the amount of which depends on chemical constitution, and not on colour. I fetched Carlyle from Chelsea to hear the lecture.

13*th February.*—To breakfast with Lacaita at his rooms in Piccadilly, opposite Burlington House. Met Sir John Acton, Arthur Russell, Grant Duff. As we were breaking up to go away we agreed to do it again, and to try and found a new little club, to breakfast together at stated intervals at each other's houses. A couple of days afterwards the same party came to breakfast in Montagu Square, with the addition of Sir Edmund Head, Sir John Lefevre, and Froude, who had been asked to join us, and "The Breakfast Club" was founded, with the very simple rules that it should consist of not more than twelve members, to breakfast together on Saturdays, at half-past nine o'clock, and as nearly as might be once a fortnight during the sitting of Parliament. Choice of new members to be unanimous, and that distinguished foreigners, not resident in England, might be invited to the breakfasts of the club. We met next time at Sir John Lefevre's house in Spring Gardens, when Lord Dufferin was invited to join us. Then at Grant Duff's in Queen's Gate Gardens, and again at Sir Edmund Head's in Eaton Square, when Bruce (now Lord Aberdare) was elected a member; and at the following meeting at Froude's house in Onslow Gardens, Sir John Simeon was added to our numbers. On the last Saturday in June all the members met at Lord Dufferin's villa at Highgate, and breakfasted *al fresco* under a tree in the garden. It was at first intended that the conversation at the breakfasts should chiefly turn on foreign literature, but this understanding was soon dropped, and the talk became general. Early in 1867 Sir Thomas Erskine May was invited to join the club, completing the full number of twelve, and from him and Sir John Lefevre we always had, in addition to other subjects, the latest news from both houses of Parliament; but party politics in general were, by a sort of tacit agreement, excluded. A remarkable point in the history of the Breakfast Club has been the way in which great offices and titles came to its members. Lord Dufferin was appointed Governor-General of Canada, and afterwards Ambassador to St. Petersburg, and Viceroy of India. Grant Duff became Governor of Madras, and Lord Reay (elected in 1879) Governor of Bombay. The Marquis of Lansdowne (elected in 1872) became Governor-General of Canada. Mr. Goschen became Chancellor of the Exchequer after his election. Lord Dufferin obtained a step in the peerage; Acton, Bruce, and Erskine May were created peers; and other honours have devolved upon members of the club.

59 MONTAGU SQUARE,<br>
27th February 1866.

MY DEAR FATHER—I have been hoping for some opportunity of seeing you before the Circuit, but as your first Commission day is to-morrow I must write to mention a book which I think will interest you. It is called *Ecce Homo*, and is published by Macmillan, now in a second edition, author unknown, but ascribed in turn to almost every writer of celebrity. It is in many ways a very remarkable book; an attempt, so to speak, to construct an *à priori* scheme of Christianity, and then to show how it agrees with the actual and historical scheme, without employing a single term of technical theology, and written in a style which is as noteworthy as the matter which it clothes.

I know you buy all books you read, whether you do or do not read all books you buy, and I commend this book to you in the knowledge and recollection of your custom, feeling that, whatever may be your ultimate opinion on it, you will not regret having made acquaintance with it.

I see the accounts of the Master of Trinity are a little better to-day. In the event, however, of a vacancy, I trust that the selection of the Crown may fall on the right man to succeed him, who is unquestionably Thompson, now Regius Professor of Greek.—Yours affectionately,   W. F. P.

HATTON, 28*th February* 1866.

MY DEAR FRED—I shall order the book, and take it with me on the Circuit. Some such book I have expected for months. Astronomy put down the infallibility of Rome. Geology and science must in like manner put down Bibliolatry, and something like a new system of belief must begin. While science renders some outworks (supposed to be) of faith untenable, it supplies others which give support to a more enlarged belief in the goodness of the Creator and the immortality of those who have been so formed as to understand His works—to look back and forward, and in a humble sense to comprehend enough to worship and adore. Everything is a revelation, if we could read it aright, and the history of the world (as we know it) is not at all inconsistent with the Christian revelation viewed in the simplicity of its first appearance. I have lately been looking again into Pusey's last work, his *Eirenicon*. How he smites the Romish Church "*hip and thigh*," and puts together, in strange contrast, the infallible nonsense and trash which have gone forth from the pretended oracle of truth!

I was sorry to hear of Whewell's accident. He must be past seventy, and at that age it is no trifle to have a concussion of the brain that suspends intelligence for twenty-four hours and upwards. You had once a trifling concussion, but it created only a momentary confusion; you spoke and recognised everybody, but you had forgotten your fall, and could not conceive why you were in Guildford Street, etc. etc. You had my library as a bedroom for about a week, and I believe perfectly recovered; but I should be afraid that Whewell's fall may give rise to future mischief.—Yours ever affectionately, FRED. POLLOCK.

*2d March.*—George Scharf lectured at the Royal Institution on the Exhibition of National Portraits at South Kensington held this year. No man was better qualified to treat of this subject, from his own knowledge of art and from his special study of it in connection with portraiture. The first collection of portraits ended with the reign of James II., and was followed by a second, beginning with the reign of William and Mary and coming down to the year 1800; while a third in 1808 continued the series down to 1867, and contained some older pictures which had not found their places in either of the earlier exhibitions. I was a frequent visitor, as I have since been to the National Portrait Gallery, while it was located in the same rooms at South Kensington, and I contributed papers to *Fraser's Magazine* in the form of dialogues on the pictures shown in each year. I am pleased to know that my friend Scharf considered them worthy of being placed in his official library as Director of the National Portrait Gallery, which I trust (writing in 1887) may speedily find a permanent and secure building for its reception. But in the meanwhile I do not regret that the people of the East End of London should have the portraits for a time placed among them in their temporary abode at Bethnal Green. For a walk among them affords one of the most useful and delightful ways in which both history and biography can be learned, and is very likely to create a taste for the study of these subjects which might not otherwise exist.

HOME CIRCUIT,<br>
*Friday, 2d March* 1866.

MY DEAR FRED—In my way to the station (King's Cross) I called at Willis's on Wednesday and bought the book. I am near the end of it. It is the most wonderful and extraordinary work I ever met with. It is a view of Christianity (without doctrine) from a particular point—the most original and comprehensive that one can conceive—startling at first by novelty and boldness, but beyond measure attractive by its genius, and so full of the true spirit and beauty of Christianity that if Festus had read it instead of hearing St. Paul, he would have said, *Altogether thou persuadest me to be a Christian.* I think it cannot be written by a clergyman of the Church of England—I should say by no "*Professor of Divinity*" in any form. The author is a learned man, of great powers, able to deal with very large questions, and still very accurate and successful in working out details. It is an astonishing production.

It is not what I expected, but I must say far better. Its goodness is even more attractive than its genius is overwhelming. Its great tendency is to prove the truth of Christianity from the whole history of the world; to show that it is "the stone cut out without hands" which is becoming a great mountain and filling the earth. I sat yesterday till five, and got through half the business, and shall easily finish to-day.—Yours affectionately,

FRED. POLLOCK.

HOME CIRCUIT,
*5th March* 1866.

MY DEAR FRED—The writer of *Ecce Homo* seems to me willing to throw a sort of veil over every vice and crime as far as he can, and excuse (not justify) much of wrong and evil by the habits and manners of the times in which they occurred; but I recollect nothing in the book that would lead me to think he could have played the part of

Calvin in the tragedy of Servetus. Stern duty does not seem to be the form in which moral excellence presents itself to his mind; but "doing good," " relieving the distressed," "caring for the poor and afflicted," "comforting the widow and the fatherless," in short, promoting happiness by every kind of self-denial and active humanity. I doubt whether he will turn out to be what they call orthodox. Obviously he puts (I think rightly) morality before doctrine, that is, obedience to the laws of Christ (as given to his subjects) from loyalty to his kingdom he puts before any opinion about the constitution or the politics of Christianity. I expect he will consider the office of Christ rather that of Mediator than of scapegoat, who produced *at-one ment* (*reconciliation*) but did not vicariously suffer punish-ment. But I must conclude, with best love to J—— and W——, not forgetting Moss, yourself, etc. F. P.

*5th March.*—We had a reading of the *Merchant of Venice*, in which my wife, Brookfield, young Herman Merivale, and W—— took the principal parts. My wife was the Portia, and Brookfield, who is a born actor, and should have played his part on the stage rather than in the pulpit, good as he was there also, made an admirable Shylock. There came as audience the Belpers, W. M. Jameses, Watsons, De Mussys, Robert Bells, Thackerays, F. D. Maurice, Spedding, G. Richmond, Edward Bunbury, Tyndall, and a few others.

11*th March.*—Drive to see Henry Taylors at East Sheen.

16*th March.*—Thompson, now in his right place as Master of Trinity, and Spedding to dinner.

Hatton, 21*st March* 1866.

My dear Fred—Nobody knows the quantity of paper I have wasted in my time. When I took my degree I had fifteen or sixteen books of MS., of which one only (like Job's messengers) remains. The rest are dispersed. I agree with you as to the propriety of recording any fact or truth in science. I remember Sir Joseph Banks told me, above fifty years ago—If you find out a new mode of making a blue colour, if the blue is not brighter or better, or the mode cheaper, it is not worth notice. *Secus* in Science; then every new truth should be recorded. Till Newton discovered the system of the world, conic sections were interesting only from their beautiful geometry (it is lovely), but it now turns out that the answer to all questions in what Cambridge people call *the branches* turns on a conic section. I should offer the matter to the Royal Society, asking Professor Stokes, the secretary, if they wanted it, and if they did, I would send it. I am not without hopes of making out some proof. It would then be very interesting.

The letter then goes on to discuss a property of prime numbers, upon which the Chief Baron was for some time much occupied.

I am amazingly delighted at F——'s success, chiefly as a proof of his general ability, and as showing that it is not

mere book work, but that mental power, capacity to think, and to think hard and well, is at the bottom of his success.
—Yours affectionately, FRED. POLLOCK.

*12th April.*—Reading of *Twelfth Night.* Brookfield, Valentia Donne, F——, W——. As Inspector of Schools in the Educational Department of the Privy Council, Brookfield used to set subjects for a short theme to be written on a slate, to test the general intelligence of the pupils. In the year of the comet of 1861, he gave it as a subject, and got the following from a girl: " Comets are very good things; they are beautiful to look at, and have long tails. They are very useful in giving people something to talk about, and we should get on very badly without comets."

*21st April.*—To dine and sleep at Anthony Trollope's at Waltham. Here he lived for some years in an old-fashioned red-brick house of about William the Third's time, with a good staircase and some large rooms in it, and standing in equally old-fashioned grounds, which served as the suggestion for the scene of my first dialogue in *Fraser's Magazine* on the portraits at South Kensington. There was a *corps de logis* and two wings, one of which held the stables in which Trollope's hunters were lodged, and the other was converted into an office for the Post Office clerks who were under him in his work of superintending the cross-post arrangements of the eastern counties. The Arthur Russells were in the house at the same time with us, and there was a dinner-party of neighbours, during which Trollope mentioned his habit of regularly writing a certain fixed amount of the novel in progress during two or three hours of the early morning, and he named the number of foolscap sheets of paper which he filled every day. I at once, to his astonishment, said, "Then you must write so many hundred words daily."—"How can you tell that?" he cried, for I was very nearly right in my guess. I did not trouble the company at the moment with the mystery of law stationers' folios of seventy-two words—with which I had to be familiar in taxing legal costs—but explained to Trollope afterwards how easy it was for me, knowing his handwriting, to make a rough computation of the number of words he would place on a sheet of paper of known size. His manner of writing a novel was thoroughly methodical. Before commencing it he would settle its length, and assign so many days to writing it, at so many words a day. Every morning the appointed portion for the day would be duly put on paper, and the day marked out, in a section of the calendar prepared for the purpose, as the days are by schoolboys to show how nearly their holidays are approaching. Without fail or mistake the novel was always finished in this way upon the exact date previously fixed for its completion. Trollope's writing for the press was very distinct and regular, and entirely free from alterations or additions, etc. It seemed to have flowed from his pen like clear liquor from a tap. When he went, I think for the first time, to Australia he asked me to correct the proofs of one of his shorter tales—*The Golden Lion of Grandpère*—but there was really nothing for me to do.

*13th June.*—C. C. S. dinner at Richmond— I in chair. Thirty dined—Lord Talbot de Malahide, Houghton, Horsman, Spencer Walpole, Venables, F. D. Maurice, Tom Taylor, Dean Alford, Robert Monteith, etc. F——'s first appearance at the dinner. It was the time of the "Cave" in politics, out of which

Horsman made much amusement. There came an excuse from Tennyson couched as follows:—

"Dear P.
Can't come.
A. T."

*3d July.*—Evening at the Deanery, Westminster. The Jerusalem chamber was open to the company. Sir Henry Holland told me that he once had a wager with Lord Nugent about Shakespeare's mention of dogs. Lord N. maintained that Shakespeare nowhere showed any fondness for dogs. Sir Henry said there were passages which showed the contrary, but that he could not find them, and paid his guinea to Lord N. I said that I thought the description of his hounds by Theseus in the *Midsummer Night's Dream* could not have been written by a man who did not care for dogs, and that Lord N. did not deserve to win his bet. Then there is Launce's dog introduced as a favourite, and nowhere anything to show that Shakespeare did not like dogs.

*9th July.*—My father resigned his place as Chief Baron, and a fortnight afterwards his baronetcy was gazetted; and by a fortuitous coincidence, in the same gazette in which it was officially announced, my brother Charles's appointment as one of Her Majesty's Counsel appeared.

*11th July.*—Dined J. E. Dorington's, Queen's Square, Westminster. Met Samuel Baker, of the Nile. I asked him about the British captives in Abyssinia. He said they would never be given up without a ransom. I replied, " Then they do not accept the *civis Romanus sum* of Lord Palmerston in Abyssinia." He said, " They care nothing about the *civis Romanus*, but they would accept the *sum.*"

*12th July.*—Henry Taylor at breakfast, after dining and sleeping in Montagu Square. Quoted from a report of the British Consul at Porto Rico, on the condition of the Chinese immigrant labourers : " They are worked hard, but not treated like slaves ; and if ill-used, they have their redress in their own hands—*by cutting their own throats."*

*6th September.*—To Bournemouth, where we occupied a house for some weeks, rejoicing much in the close neighbourhood of Sir Henry and Lady Taylor and their family. Henry

Taylor once spent an evening with S. T. Coleridge, in company with Charles Lamb. There was a long argument between Coleridge and Taylor, in which Taylor defended Mahometanism. In coming away, when they were looking for their hats, Lamb said to Henry Taylor, "You seem not able to find your *turban.*"

CHALDON, BOURNEMOUTH,<br>15*th September* 1866.

MY DEAR FATHER—I have not yet seen the new Latin Primer, but your mention of it, together with the buzz of controversy going on in the newspapers, have induced me to write for it. I have also written to Huntingford to inquire if he knows whether it will be adopted in the public schools, as I am responsible for M——'s Latin a few months longer, and if the drill is to be changed the sooner we get out of the old into the new the better. This proves an agreeable place. In form it is peculiar. It lies in a sinus of land fronting a spacious bay of the sea—the view, bounded on the E. by the Isle of Wight, looking right into Alum Bay, and on the W. by the point which shuts out Swanage. The town may be described as a resolvable nebula or cluster of villas, each in its own garden. There are no streets, rows, terraces, squares, crescent, or other forms of continuous bricks and mortar. All the houses are on a good scale—calculated for Dives, or his wife and daughters, if afflicted with weak lungs. A few crumbs of health are tossed to Lazarus, who is represented by twenty or thirty patients in a convalescent hospital called the Sanatorium. But for genteel Phthisis, with a large family and a limited income, there is no provision. The place, however, is in rapid development, and when the railroad reaches it no doubt will lose its present plutocratic aspect. Some day it will be one of the largest watering-places in England—a kind of Cheltenham-super-mare.

I see that an experiment has been made of lighting Hyde Park at night from a lime-light placed on a lofty pillar in the middle. Anything is desirable that would obviate the necessity of laying gas-pipes in that virgin soil, but the law of the inverse square of the distance is unfavourable to illumination from a single centre.

I spent the evening with Carlyle on the day that I had been with you at the National Gallery. He mentioned the letter you had written in reply to a request to join the Eyre Defence Committee, to which there have not been very many important adhesions. Sir James Clark has since been added, and I suppose would not have suffered his name to appear if it had been unacceptable to the Queen.

Henry Taylor is disposed to support Eyre in all he did, including the extermination of Gordon; but what Eyre now seems chiefly to want is to be saved from his more indiscreet friends.—Yours affectionately, W. F. P.

HATTON, 16*th September* 1866.

MY DEAR FRED—The new primer was, I understand, patronised and adopted by *all* the *great* schools, *public and private*. *One* system, no doubt, must be the *best* with respect to every matter in the business of life; but there are many matters in which the *best* for any *given* individual is *that* which he has been *accustomed to*, and the best (*abstractedly*) is not so *much better* as to make it *worth changing*. This is true of many personal, social, and domestic habits, and I should have thought it true of a Latin grammar, with reference to learning Latin. A grammar is certainly not necessary to learn your own language, and although I think more accurate scholars are made by the grammatical than the Hamiltonian method, I think the question which grammar should be used is not sufficiently important to disturb the teaching of thousands of boys who are half-way through one grammar, and compel them to take up another. I am sorry for Moss.

With respect to Eyre, I wish you had told me (if *you had anything to tell*) what Carlyle said about my answer; but for the *name of Carlyle* on the committee, I think I should have returned no answer at all. I think it is clear that a judge of Westminster Hall would be quite out of place on such a committee; and as I had not left the bench more than a few days when I was asked to join it, I thought it scarcely decent to ask me; but being still a member of the Court of Appeal from Jamaica, I thought it would be *most indecent* to say *Yes*, and I hope Carlyle did not discommend my saying *No*. I am disposed to agree entirely with Henry Taylor. When such a community as the white inhabitants of Jamaica are threatened with a murderous extermination, the Governor, whose duty it is to save them, must not be over-nice; he must be sure that his measures will succeed. Given that there was an extensive plot to produce insurrection (about which all seem agreed, and there seems to be no doubt), and that the outbreak was the beginning of its active development, Eyre was justified in everything he did. A captain of a man-of-war who observes a mutinous spirit in his crew is justified in shooting the first man who disobeys him, and it is *humanity* to put down mutiny by great severity. But there is a pusillanimity in modern statesmen which is really fearful: people who honestly and sincerely think reform dangerous are afraid to say so. Instead of asking what it is *right* to do, the question put is, "What will people say?" One of the great merits of Carlyle (he has many) is the courage with which he states any opinion which he has sincerely formed. I am glad to see what you say of Sir J. Clark. One may take it for granted that he knows it will not be offensive to the Queen, and how should it? When you are extinguishing a fire, ought you to be very nice about wetting the bystanders? This day week I enter my eighty-fourth year, and I have every reason to be very thankful that so much is left of me. I think I may venture to hope to share in the *Equitable* division of 1870. The affairs of the world are becoming more interesting every day. Since '52 America has put down civil war, and Prussia has swallowed up North Germany. One cannot help asking, "What'll be next?"—besides having discovered that clay is a noble metal, and that magnesium gives such a light. Love to J——, etc.—Yours affectionately, F. P.

BOURNEMOUTH, 26*th September* 1866.

MY DEAR FATHER—I am very glad to find that you have quite decided not to sit at the Privy Council. I do not think that the public has any reasonable claim upon you for further services, and it would be very much in contradiction to the considerations that had weight with those who care for you in desiring your retirement that you should not be relieved from all further official labour.

Carlyle's *Life of Sterling* will do more towards securing Sterling's future reputation than any of his own remains. He would not have been forgotten so long as any personal recollection or tradition of him continued in force, but his writings alone would not suffice to keep his fame alive. He was very great in conversation, the most remarkable person in that way whom I have known. The first time I saw him he was in the chair at the dinner of a Cambridge society to which I belong, and he then acquitted himself with much eloquence, and made the occasion as interesting as possible. His being in orders was a mistake. You will have seen from the *Life* that Hare was answerable for this. He thought that by committing him to ordination his orthodoxy would be secured. Sterling was far too able and honest to be permanently secured within the desired confines of thought by having to wear a black coat and white tie, and fortunately did not take the next step, which would have rendered it more difficult for him to fall back into the ranks of the laity. W—— and I made an excursion yesterday to Portland, with an order from the Home Office. The name procured much attention and courtesy from the Governor of the convict prison, which is well worth seeing. There is no horror, no romance in English prison life, no dungeons, or crawling reptiles, or black bread. But the enforced regularity of good food, cleanliness, and comfort, with the silence and seclusion, must be appalling to the criminal classes. We were told that the convicts now come from a far lower class than formerly, in fact almost entirely from the neglected dregs of the population, who form the dangerous element in our large towns, and whose existence is so great a disgrace to the country. They work fairly—not as much as paid labourers—but enough to earn the value of £50,000 per annum of wages at the usual rate, which is so much saved to the public in their keep. Roupell is the lion convict. He was in immediate attendance in the Governor's ante-room, as a sort of clerk. He had to rise and make a profound salutation as we passed in and out, wearing the same dress as the rest—which is as absurd and grotesque as it is humiliating. This was the only really painful sight. The gangs at work in the quarries looked well in health and not unhappy. The prison is on the highest part of the rock, and we were allowed to return by the incline down which the stone goes to the breakwater. From this the view of Weymouth Bay and the breakwater is very fine.—Yours affectionately,

W. F. P.

*7th November.* — At dinner, Houghton, Tyndall, MacGregor (canoe), Herman Merivale, Froude.

*13th November.*—This was the day on which the great shower of shooting stars was predicted to appear. We had been dining with the Martins in Eaton Square, but took care to be at home in time to see the exhibition from its commencement. At the appointed time the first shooting star rose like a rocket from behind the opposite houses. Every minute they became more and more frequent, until the whole visible sky seemed sometimes to be full of trains of light. It was a racing and chasing in silence of rapid, fiery meteors, with sharp and sudden dartings hither and thither, and wonderful combinations of splendid outbursts and speedy extinctions, and all transacted with a prodigious stillness in the midst of so much visible commotion. At last, about twelve o'clock, we thought we could vary the point of observation with advantage, and see the display better away from the street lights, if we went up to the Toxophilite Ground in the Regent's Park. Edward Herries was staying with us, and, hastily putting on whatever wraps and hats came first to hand in the hall, we sallied forth with him in a state of considerable emotion and excitement. In passing through the streets on our way to the Park, it was strange to note that no one was deriving the same pleasure as we were from the wonderfully grand and beautiful spectacle that was being performed in the sky. Not a window was open, not a person was on the look-out in the streets. When we got to the gate of the ground I began ringing the bell to wake Percy, the gardener, who lived in the lodge, to get him up to let us in. While I was so occupied a policeman came up and asked what we were doing, and I daresay that our odd costumes and manner may have justified some suspicions of our intentions. I answered, "Oh, we are only come here to get away from the gas lights," and the constable rejoined, "So I thought. You don't look as if you were the sort as likes gas." Further trouble and explanation were saved by the appearance of Percy with the key, and we were not asked any more questions. By this time the meteors had begun to diminish in numbers, but we certainly did see them better away from the gas, and returned home, after warming ourselves by the stove in the Archers' Hall, by half-past two, full of the joy of having witnessed the magnificent sight of this memorable night.

*2d December.*—My father gave me a portion of the collar of S. S. worn by him as Chief Baron—one of the knots and one S, to make a pendant ornament for my wife, and one of the portcullises, of which the chain contained three, for myself. The whole collar was broken up, and portions also given to other members of the family.

LONDON, *9th December* 1866.

MY DEAR FATHER—J—— tells me that you are much interested in the (so-called) mask of Shakespeare, now in the keeping of Owen, and lately seen by you. I saw it, and had the opportunity of examining it very carefully when it first came to this country some years ago. It was then in the possession of König, in his private residence at the British Museum, having been sent there from Germany with a view to its purchase by the British nation.

The only tradition which I remember to have heard

mentioned as connecting the cast with Shakespeare, was that it had at one time been in the collection of a German savant, who was an admirer of S., and who believed it to be a cast from his face. But, as far as I recollect, this did not carry it very far back, and there was no trace of its previous history or of how it got into this gentleman's museum. As to the evidence presented by the thing itself, it is, no doubt, a genuine cast from the human face, and probably taken after death. It bears the probably contemporaneous mark of the year in which S. died; and the external indications of brain-power are of a very rare and high power. Nor are the features so unlike those which are received as Shakespeare's as to exclude the possibility of the cast having been actually taking from his face, although there is no evidence (that I am aware of) of this cast having been taken in England at all.

On the other hand, it must be remarked that many persons besides S. died in 1616, and notably Cervantes (both on the 23d April 1616), æt. sixty-nine—an age to which I should (from my recollections) be more inclined to refer the original of the cast than to S., who died at fifty-two. The features, too, might pass as well for Cervantes as for S. But, without seeking for a possible original among the illustrious deceased of 1616, it must be borne in mind that it was then usual for persons of condition to be represented after death by funeral and monumental effigies, for which purpose it would be desirable (as now for busts) to take a cast from the face after death. It has always been held that the bust at Stratford-on-Avon was founded on such a cast. This, as you know, is very coarsely executed, probably by some country stone-mason, but I do not think that any sculptor would recognise the model for it in the German cast, after making every fair allowance for divergence in execution.

Such a cast, too, found in Germany is *à priori* more likely to have been taken from some one on the Continent than in England. In the absence of any pedigree, and of any cogent confirmation from personal resemblance, the case in favour of the mask's being a cast from S. rests only upon its apparent genuineness as a cast taken from some one after death in the year 1616. It is, from the grandeur of its conformation, more likely to have been taken from a great man than otherwise, and the circumstance of its careful preservation (unless handed down in a family, of which there is no evidence) tends to show that it was connected with some well-known great man, and that man may have been Shakespeare.

The cast created much interest at the time it was at the British Museum, and was seen by all the Shakespearean scholars and dilettanti, but without (as far as I know) producing any conviction that it really was what it was shown for. We are going to Cambridge for a couple of days to stay at Trinity Lodge, and shall see F—— receive some prizes in Hall—for first class in College Examination, a Declamation cup, and for an English essay.—Yours affectionately, W. F. P.

*12th December.*—To Trinity Lodge, to stay with the Master and Mrs. Thompson. Brookfields also there. The following day was that of the College Commemoration. In the morning to chapel for the commemoration service, at which Monro preached, and then to the hall for the distribution of prizes, and to hear W. K. Clifford deliver his oration as winner of the first Declamation prize. It was in this oration that Clifford gave an apologue of the Trilobites, who lived in a glimmering light at the bottom of an ancient ocean, to illustrate the history of scientific discovery and religious persecution. An enterprising trilobite got to the surface, saw the sun, and reported it as the source of their light. He was at once put to death as an innovator and a heretic. Afterwards another trilobite went up at night, saw the moon, and announced it as a second source of light. The belief in the sun had in the meantime become current and was tolerated, and at last became an article of orthodox belief; but, again, the moon was a novelty, and the new discoverer was in his turn put to death. In course of time, however, both sun and moon got accepted, and a trilobite was thought very ignorant who did not believe in both of them.

*15th January* 1867.—Anthony Trollopes to dine and sleep. At dinner W. Rathbone Greg, Froude, Charles Herries. Next morning when Trollope came down to breakfast, after having been writing the novel then on hand, as usual, he rather astonished us by saying, " I have just been making my twenty-seventh proposal of marriage."

*5th June.*—C. C. S. dinner at Richmond—Hardcastle in chair. Houghton, Sir Arthur Buller, Spedding, F. Garden, etc.

*11th June.*—To Cambridge. Lunch No. 1 at Trinity Lodge. To giving of medals, prizes, etc., in Senate House. Lunch No. 2 with Vice-Chancellor (Cartmel) at Christ's Lodge.

*24th June.*—Dine with Venables at Oxford and Cambridge Club. R. Monteith, F. Garden, Sir John Simeon, Aubrey de Vere, W. Vernon Harcourt, F. Lushington, Doyle.

*11th July.*—Dined with Theodore Martins. Dean of Westminster and Lady Augusta Stanley, Froudes, Helps, R. Browning, Venables, Col. Hamley, Mrs. Procter.

*20th July.*—Club breakfast at home. Motley as a guest. He was again with us at the next meeting of the Club at Erskine May's, from which I took him to see the Record Office. He was much gratified by the rapid production at his request of a particular despatch of some importance in the history of the American war of independence, which he asked to see. The same afternoon I had a walk with Carlyle, when the conversation turned on the devotion of Spedding's life to the study and rehabilitation of Bacon. Carlyle said, "When I used to go to the British Museum I always saw a round white object over papers on a table, and this was the head of him." Then he went on to say that the importance of Bacon's place in the history of science was much over-rated. In this I agreed, and added that I thought Kepler's work had not been sufficiently recognised in this country. Carlyle looked at me with surprise, and asked with some kind of scorn what I knew about Kepler. I was able to let him see that I was not altogether uninformed about Kepler, and he became very gracious again.

*3d August.*—Stories of Lord Chief Justice Ellenborough. He once came rushing out from a debate in the House of Lords and ran against the Prince of Wales, for which he apologised, "I beg your Royal Highness's pardon, but I am responsible to my Creator for the use of my time, and Lord Darnley is speaking."

Lord Westmoreland was on his legs in the House of Lords, and, giving his opinion on the question in debate, said, "My Lords, at this point I asked myself a question. . . ." Lord Ellenborough, in a loud aside, "And a d—d stupid answer you'd be sure to get to it."

*13th August.*—Motley came to dine. He was very good at this time in coming to see my wife, who was not well. On one occasion I went downstairs to the house door with him, and said, "You see I treat you with diplomatic ceremony, in anticipation of your coming to London as American minister." He replied, "That is out of the question. Vienna was all very well, but I have been too many years away from America to be thought of for London." I said, "We shall see."

*25th August.*—On this day died Faraday. A great and good man gone. At the request of Mrs. Faraday the account of his life, which appeared soon afterwards in the *Illustrated London News*, was written by my wife and myself. After the publication of Dr. Bence Jones's *Life of Faraday* there were articles upon it by my wife in *St. Paul's Magazine* for June 1870, and by myself in *Fraser's Magazine* for March 1871.

*6th September.*—To Paris with Donne and

his daughter Valentia for a little tour in Switzerland—Basle, Lucerne, Rigi, Pilatus, Gründelwald, Berne, Chillon, Neufchâtel, Dijon.

LONDON, 15*th November* 1867.

MY DEAR FATHER—I have finished the Parkes-Merivale volumes, and one opinion excited is that the last editor has hardly given time enough to his work. But there is some excuse in the rather obsolete nature of the principal subject of interest supposed to be connected with Francis, and an enormous mass of papers, already mammocked and much tumbled over, some of them over and over again, must be very repulsive. Hayward is taking up the cudgels against the Franciscan theory, and, no doubt, there is still plenty of room for ingenious argument, although there is, as I think, no reasonable moral doubt that Sir Philip Francis was the man, remote as it still is from absolutely conclusive proof. If he succeeds in shaking the accepted belief, I shall then come out with my theory that Junius was George the Third. The recent publication of his letters to Lord North has done much to set him up, and this will do more. —Yours affectionately, W. F. P.

*7th December.*—The registering thermometer outside a window, looking east, at the Athenæum Club showed this morning a difference of nearly a hundred degrees between the maximum and minimum temperature of the night, and the minimum was not far from the freezing point. The great fire which destroyed Her

Majesty's Theatre in the Haymarket had occurred during the night. A pane of glass in a window of the drawing-room, a few yards nearer to the source of heat, was cracked.

# CHAPTER VI

### MONTALEMBERT

*7th January* 1868.—Dined with Merivales. Kinglake, Leslie Stephen, Annie Thackeray. Kinglake had an anecdote of Montalembert and his tenants during an election under the Second Empire in France. He desired them to go and vote as he wished, against the Government. They came back without having voted. He asked, " Pourquoi n'avez vous pas voté ?"—" Mais, Monsieur le Comte, il y avaient des gensdarmes."—" Qu'est ce qu'ils ont fait ?" " Rien, Monsieur le Comte."—" Qu'est ce qu'ils ont dit."—" Rien, Monsieur le Comte." " Mais pourquoi donc . . . ?"—" Ils y étaient, Monsieur le Comte."

*8th January.*—Dined with William Spottiswoodes. Goschen, Frederick Harrison, Bonamy Price, etc.

*21st January.*—Performance of *Castle Rummelsberg* at 59 Montagu Square. This was an original piece, founded on the German tale of the Spectre Barber, written by my wife, and "licensed" for performance by Donne, at this time the Examiner of Plays in the Lord Chamberlain's office. He was himself so kind as to take a small part under the *nom de theatre* of Mr. Bodham (his own second name). His daughter Valentia played in the piece as Miss Chamberlain; the other characters were sustained by my wife and our sons.

*6th February.*—With a view to the better ventilation of the lecture theatre at the Royal Institution, I went over Spottiswoode's printing office and the lecture-room of the Chemical Society at Burlington House, and made experiments in company with Frankland and De la Rue. B. L. Chapman showed me, at the request of Tennyson, a proposed contract with Moxon & Co. for a library edition of his poems in four volumes, which we determined to advise him not to accept, as not being favourable for him to the extent it ought to be.

*10th February.*—To Beresford Hope's London committee, on the contest with Cleasby for the seat for the University of Cambridge vacated by Selwyn's elevation to the bench.

*22d February* 1868.

MY DEAR FATHER—You may be amused to hear that your voting paper was not allowed to pass muster at the polling at Cambridge, as you did not describe yourself as Jonathan Frederick, under which names you appear on the register. One vote, however, is now of no consequence. The numbers at one o'clock to day were—Hope, 1789; Cleasby, 1300—so that winning looks easy.

*22d February.*—Breakfast at Sir John Lefevre's. Dufferin, Grant Duff, Lacaita, Acton, Froude, Erskine May, Simeon, Bruce. Lady Acton (grandmother of Sir John) is now alive, aged eighty. Her husband was born in 1730, the same year in which Gibbon was born. He was minister to the King of Naples. She was his niece, and was sent for from England to marry her uncle, under a Papal dispensation, in order to continue the family. On her arrival at Naples she remembers talking to an officer who had been in the service of Louis XIV. (who died in 1715), accompanying a Neapolitan contingent to the French army.

*23d February.*—To the Rolls Chapel to hear Brookfield preach. He was always very delightful to listen to in the pulpit, and full of varied illustrations from life and literature. The chapel was an extremely quiet place to go to, and at this time the pew of the Master of the Rolls projected into it with an oriel window, the sashes of which required to be opened in order to hear the service and sermon. It communicated with one of the rooms in the house of the Master of the Rolls, and must have afforded a luxurious way of going to church for him to hear himself specially prayed for, as was done at the Rolls Chapel in the Bidding prayer before the sermon, used in that place as at the Universities. After service, to lunch with the Flowers at the College of Surgeons in Lincoln's Inn Fields, and went over the Museum, for which he is doing so much. Dined with Bergenroth at Ford's Hotel; met Acton and W. C. Cartwright, who afterwards wrote a life of Bergenroth, a remarkable, learned, and interesting man, who, after some European adventures, had a strange career as a sort of independent sovereign in South America, and latterly had been employed by our Record Office in historical researches at Simancas. During his stay in London he was an invited guest at the

Athenæum Club, and it was said that he and Strzelecki used to spend a good deal of time in fruitless conversation together, each trying to discover the precise nationality of the other.

*1st March.* — Dine Sir John Simeon's. Matthew Arnold, Bergenroth, Arthur Russell, Mrs. Dunlop.

*5th March.* — Anthony Trollopes staying with us. At dinner Sir Frederick and Lady Rogers, Lacaita, Dr. De Mussy, Julia Moore.

*7th March.* — At dinner Mrs. Cameron, Arthur Russells, S. Laurence, Bergenroth, Lecky.

*10th March.* — My father was at this time much interested in the scheme for placing appropriate statues of eminent men on the front of the new building for the London University in Burlington Gardens, and I received the following letter from him :—

HATTON, *10th March* 1868.

MY DEAR FRED—I send you a printed paper giving an account of twenty-two statues to be put up at the University of London. I am shocked at Shakespeare being left out, and Milton made to represent Law, Medicine, Arts, and Sciences, he having nothing to do with any of the four. I grieve to see Lucretius put in, Homer and Horace unnoticed. I object to Galen instead of Hippocrates, and Priestley as a chemist instead of Sir Humphry Davy.

In a letter of the same date to Dr. Sharpey he urged the claims of Sir Humphry Davy to be represented, and pointed out that Cavendish in England and Lavoisier in France were at least the equals of Priestley, but that no one but Faraday could at all be put in competition with Davy. He strongly protested against the omission of Shakespeare, as the mightiest genius ever produced by England or any other country, whose language and expressions are unconsciously used by every one who speaks English, whether in speeches in the senate or familiar talk in the pot-house, and whose finest passages have passed into household words. A student at a university had better read Shakespeare than the works of any or all the twenty-two persons selected. If the proper study of mankind is man, Shakespeare is worth all other authors put together, but at the University of London he is ignored.

I replied to my father :—

59 Montagu Square,<br>
10th March 1868. 10 P.M.

My dear Father—I agree with you that the subjects selected for the statues at the new building for the U. of London are not the right ones, but I think I can understand upon what grounds the choice has been made. Literature, as unconnected with *instruction*, is probably not intended to be represented, but, even on this ground, Shakespeare should not have been excluded. The great poet of the land, and the great founder of its modern language, ought surely to be honoured in any place of *English education*, and as such should occupy the place now given to Milton.

Milton, as a representative of education, is on his own merits entitled to be somewhere, in a very high place, but not in the highest. He was a man of vast power and accomplishment, and his views of education were far in advance of his age. With Newton and Harvey one cannot quarrel, and I suppose Bentham is right. I do not like all the names in the next series. Aristotle—*il maestro di color che sanno*—is right, and Plato, as representing a large part of Greek philosophy. Lucretius, in a purely literary point of view, is entitled to a distinguished, if not the first place in Roman literature. But he was probably selected as the author of the great exposition of the physical system of Epicurus, contained in his *De rerum naturâ*, the value of which is more and more being recognised, as it is found, though dimly and vaguely, to coincide with some of the most recent and advanced speculations in science. For Euclid I would substitute Archimedes, one of the greatest natural philosophers of any age, but not so much associated with education as Euclid. I think with you that Hippocrates is far worthier of honour than Galen, but perhaps he and Pliny were selected to make an even balance of Greek and Roman names. Pliny was a gossiping encyclopædist, credulous and altogether unscientific. His name, however, is a familiar one, and without using it there would have been a difficulty in finding three Roman names, if three were to be used.

I should have much preferred some representation of the Middle Ages, and to have taken Roger Bacon or Albertus Magnus, both eminent teachers as well as writers in their day.

But their names are not generally familiar, and would have required explanation to most people. Yet, as teachers, it can hardly be alien from the functions of the U. of London to teach in stone who are the great men who thought and taught in former times, and not merely to accept as such the popular and best recognised celebrities. In the next series, Cuvier, Leibnitz, and Linnæus must be accepted. Cuvier and Linnæus are the modern successors to the greatness of Aristotle, and both eminent as teachers as well as discoverers and organisers.

Leibnitz too, the subtlest and most varied intellect of modern ages, needs no defence.

Bacon is of course there. He, in Tennyson (copying Dante's *Aristotle*), is "The first of those who know," and he also was a great teacher.

So was Adam Smith, as founder of the modern science of Political Economy.

As to Locke, his name will never be forgotten, but some worthier representative of mental philosophy in modern times might be found, although it would be difficult to do so without resorting to men still alive or recently dead, about whom agreement could hardly be expected. In the last group Galileo and Descartes require no comment. Goethe's claims to be considered as a natural philosopher are not so generally known, but they are not trifling. He wrote an original work on the metamorphoses of plants, which materially assisted in forming the modern theory of vegetable development, and had some share in advancing the views now universally adopted of the uniformity and generality of the vertebrate type. In physical optics he was less successful, and his *Treatise on Colours* is false and fanciful. Except for his literary fame, he would probably not be now much remembered as a physicist, but I daresay the Committee were glad to be able to use a great name, only why have they not been equally solicitous about Shakespeare? I would not have both Franklin and Priestley, but should prefer the substitution of Davy for one of them. The Pope, as you know, never canonises a saint who has been dead less than a hundred years; a similar rule is convenient in dealing with all reputations for the purposes of permanent glorification. For this reason, although I believe that Faraday was the greatest experimental philosopher that ever lived, yet sufficient time has not elapsed since his death to enable general opinion to solidify to the same conviction. But Davy's fame has securely settled on its foundations, and, if not too late, a strong effort should be made to place his statue on the new building. Between Franklin and Priestley it might be hard to decide: Priestley's labours were the most varied and important, and Franklin's eminence depends a good deal on the non-scientific portions of his career. In Priestley the dissenting minister and the politician may be forgotten, but as one of the founders of the chemistry of gases his name must always be remembered.—Yours affectionately,

W. F. P.

The recommendations of the Committee appointed for the purpose were, however, reviewed by the Senate of the University of London. Cicero was substituted for Pliny, Archimedes for Euclid, and Tribonian for

Lucretius; Laplace took the place of Descartes, Shakespeare that of Johnson, and Dalton that of Priestley.

*14th March.*—Dined W. M. James. Strangfords, Henry Reeves, Countess Teleki, Edward Bunbury, De Mussy, C. Newton, Robert Browning, F. Galton.

*24th March.*—Dined Lord Belper's. Sir C. and Lady Lyell, Lecky, Spedding, Edward Romillys, E. Twisleton, Sir Edward Ryan, etc.

*28th March.*—E. Twisleton, who must have been in Dublin at the time, told a story of Lord Normanby, when Lord-Lieutenant, and Norman Macdonald, whom he one day asked to dine at the Castle on the same evening. Macdonald, presuming on his friendship with Lord Normanby, said he could not come as he had friends coming to dine with him at home. The Lord-Lieutenant asked who they were and learned their names. In the course of the afternoon Macdonald received notice from all his expected guests, excusing themselves from coming to him, as they were honoured with commands to dine at the Castle. This was a lesson in etiquette. Macdonald should have accepted the invitation, and then have craved under the circumstances to be permitted not to obey it.

*1st April.*—Dinner at home. Sir John and Lady Simeon, Henry Cowper, Mrs. Brookfield, Speddings, Flowers, Lecky, Henry Phillips.

*6th April.*—At dinner Palmer, the Oriental scholar, prestidigitateur, and altogether wonderful person, and Forrest. There was some talk about stage law: In *No Thoroughfare*—1. Diamonds bought as a present, but not accepted by the person for whom they were intended, cannot be re-converted into money; 2. Proof of personal identity is complete by inspection of a paper containing the names of persons who, several years before, could have proved the identity. In *The Hero of Romance*, taken from *Le Jeune Homme pauvre*, if an agent embezzles money belonging to his employer, and lays it out in the purchase of an estate; after the discovery of the fraud when both are dead, the estate passes *ipso facto* from the heirs of the agent to those of his employer.

*26th April.*—To see Tennyson, staying with James Knowles at Clapham. Much talk about his future publishers. Evening at Lady Simeon's.

*27th April.*—Tennyson to lunch with my wife. W. K. Clifford to dine.

*30th April.*—Dined with Knowles, Clapham Common, going there with Tyndall. Tennyson read from " Maud."

*6th May.*—Literary Fund Dinner. Disraeli was in the chair. It was remarkable that he made no allusion in his speeches to his ever having been himself concerned with literature. Venables, on my suggestion, made one of the best speeches of the evening. No one of the Committee except myself seemed to be aware of his excellence as a speaker.

*9th May.*—Visit to Cambridge. Lunch with W—— in Trinity; dine with J. W. Clark. Evening to C. C. S. at Clifford's rooms. Next day breakfast and lunch with F——, and dined with Jebb. On Monday, breakfast with Forrest in St. John's; lunched with Clifford, where Kingsley came in; five o'clock tea at Trinity Lodge; dined with Jackson. Tuesday, breakfasted with Jebb; lunched with Palmer in St. John's, where was Kingsley; and to town in afternoon.

*26th May* 1868.

My dear Fred—I have been looking over *Ecce Homo* again. Some of it is fanciful, some feeble. When I first read it I was surprised at the use he made of the Temptation. He treats it all as real and literally true. No eminent theologian has done this; I think none. The notion of its being a vision is what is generally adopted. I don't think I ever heard a sermon about it. It involves that difficult question which is a step farther than the origin of evil—Who created the devil? and why? For myself, I do not believe in any such existence, though he is mentioned in an indictment for murder. He is a figure of rhetoric, nothing more. A prosopopœia of the bad and mischievous passions of mankind. What would Carlyle say to this? I should like much to know.—Yours affectionately, Fred. Pollock.

*25th May.*—At dinner Boxall, Herman Merivale. Evening, Trenches, Speddings, Groves, Thackerays, Venables, Babbage, Watsons, Deutsch, S. Laurence, E. Bunbury, Moores, Duckworths.

*2d June.*—Breakfast with Sir Henry Holland. These breakfasts were always very interesting. The hour was early, and the guests not more than one or two. Sir Henry's talk was full of anecdote and observations on men and manners. When the ladies of his family left the room, he would ask one to stay a little longer, and continue his talk until about ten o'clock.

Dined at Athenæum with Tyndall, Hirst, and Boxall, and afterwards to Carlyle at Chelsea.

*6th June.*—Came to breakfast with me Lord Lyttelton, Sir Walter James, Robert Monteith, Aubrey de Vere, Frederick Locker.

*11th June.*—Dined Merchant Taylors' Hall. It was the Election Day Dinner, and in connection with their school a large number of bishops were present, and among them Wilberforce, then bishop of Oxford. The Duke of Wellington was to have returned thanks for the usual toast of the House of Lords, and the Bishop of Oxford for a toast of the Bench of Bishops. But the Duke was prevented from coming in consequence of an accident, and Lord Leigh, the senior temporal peer present, was substituted for him, and returned thanks accordingly. When the toast of the Bench of Bishops was reached my neighbour at dinner said to me, "Now we shall have a good speech." I replied, "I think you will not. A great mistake has been made in asking a Baron to return thanks for the House of Lords, when so many Bishops are here who take precedence of him." I was right, for the Bishop of Oxford in returning thanks merely said, "On behalf of my right reverend brethren and myself, I have to thank the company for the honour done to us by drinking our healths." Governor Eyre was a guest at the dinner, and his name was down on the list of toasts, and at that particular time many persons did not wish to show approval of his recent conduct of affairs in Jamaica by remaining to take part in drinking his health. There was accordingly a considerable rush to get away in time to avoid it, in which I joined, and just outside the hall I met the Bishop of Oxford. In his genial way he held out both hands to me and asked, "Don't you think I was right? It was for my order, and not for myself, that I resented the slight put upon us." I replied by saying that I had anticipated what he would do, but that it was very hard upon the innocent guests at large to deprive them of the pleasure of listening to a speech from him, because the officials of the company had made a blunder. He said, "That could not be avoided," and we parted. Touching after-dinner toasts in the city, I remember Sir Robert Inglis once telling me that when an undergraduate at Oxford he was in London after the Peace of

Amiens, and dined at the Mansion House. The company were invited by the Lord Mayor to do honour to the then supreme authority in France by drinking to the health of the " Three Consuls." But the toast-master, less acquainted with them than with certain things very well known in the city, and of somewhat similar sound, gave out as the toast "The Three per Cent Consols." Another time he heard the toast of "Henry the Eighth" given out by the toast-master instead of "Henry of Hayti," the sometime sovereign of that country.

*16th June.*—Dined with Beresford Hope at the Trafalgar, Greenwich, to celebrate his return as member for Cambridge University. My wife dined with the Archbishop of Dublin, where I joined her.

*1st July.*—Dined with Macmillan at Garrick Club. Met White (New York), George Grove, Dallas, Lockyer, Townsend (*Spectator*), Dr. Sadler (editor of Crabbe Robinson's *Memoirs*), Abdy, Craigie.

*3d July.*—Performance of an abridged version of *She Stoops to Conquer* at George Richmond's house, York Street. My wife was

Mrs. Hardcastle, and Fred Farrer made a capital Tony Lumpkin. The play was acted in the large room on the ground floor, which was as full as it could be, but I was chiefly "behind" and looking on from the side. About the middle of the evening Richmond quietly told me that the house had been on fire, that it had been put out, and begged me to say nothing about it. It was a warm evening and the windows were all open, so that in one of the bedrooms looking backwards a curtain had been blown against the lighted candles upon the toilet table in a window and had set light to them. The blaze was seen from outside and an alarm given, but all the servants were downstairs busy, or trying to see the play. An engine came to the front door and the firemen rang and thundered at it, but actors and spectators were all too much engrossed in the performance to hear what was going on outside. Richmond himself went up, got the fire put out, and refused to admit the firemen, and no one knew what had happened. It was a remarkable exercise of good judgment and presence of mind, for if the alarm had been communicated to the actors and audience a mischievous panic might have followed.

HATTON, 6*th July* 1868.

MY DEAR FRED—Your July number is exceedingly good (*Fraser's Magazine*, the last dialogue on the Portrait Exhibitions). I do not consider this collection of portraits the last. I think there will be one every year, or every three or four, for those departed since the last, and stray portraits which have not appeared before, of anybody and any time. It is so agreeable a mode of refreshing one's history, and improving one's biography, that having once begun it will not cease. My last paper (on the Theory of Numbers), as I learn from a letter of yesterday, is to appear in the *Philosophical Transactions*. This is very gratifying. I wrote it since I was eighty-four, and I doubt whether there be any production of so ancient a person in the whole series. . . . I have talked with some of my people about *The Spanish Gipsy*. There is amazing power and genius in it, but the story is so shocking and so utterly improbable, if not absolutely impossible, that my feelings cannot bear it, and my sense of truth and propriety rebels against anything so untruthful to nature.—Yours affectionately,

FRED. POLLOCK.

*8th July.*—To see *The Rivals* at the Queen's Theatre. Wigan was Sir Anthony Absolute, a good performance; and Mrs. Wigan made a perfect Mrs. Malaprop, letting drop her blunders in words with absolute unconsciousness. To see her in her dressing-room after the play.

*11th July.*—Dine with De Mussys. Edward Diceys, W. Spottiswoode, Benedict, W. R. Greg, Benzons.

*28th July.*—Lady Cranworth, when Miss Carr, set to music part of Wordsworth's ballad of "Young Romilly," and he heard her sing it at Lord Monteagle's house. The company were curious to see what effect it would have upon the poet. When the singing was over Wordsworth went up to Miss Carr and all he said was, "You have omitted a great deal of my poetry in your musical recitation." This I heard from Aubrey de Vere, who was present. Wordsworth was much distressed at Scott's misquotation from his "Yarrow,"

"The swans on sweet St. Mary's lake,"

instead of

"The swan on still St. Mary's lake,"

as destroying the beauty and truth of the imagery, and the propriety of the epithet. He used to say that Scott had no real feeling for nature, but that he would go out and collect impressions and versify them, "but nature cannot be inventoried in that way."

Dugald Stewart was once asked what was

the earliest thing he could remember. He said it was being left alone by his nurse in his cradle, and resolving to tell of her as soon as he could speak.

*9th September.*—Left town for Switzerland. The Henry Taylors kindly took charge of our youngest boy, M——, on a visit to them at Bournemouth, for the remainder of his holidays. We went by Paris, Dijon, and Neufchâtel to Zurich.

HOTEL BAUER AU LAC,<br>ZURICH, 20th September 1868.

MY DEAR FATHER—We give up our transalpine programme. The heat is too great to make it wise to rush into greater. This is a charming if not a very invigorating place—a large well-found hotel, where we have a room with a balcony over the water, a shady garden, baths, boats, and a fine town. Accordingly we are remaining here for a week, and to-morrow go to Berne for a night, and on Tuesday to Gründelwald, where we purpose to remain a week at least, and where a letter addressed to the *Hotel l'Aigle*, Gründelwald, will find us. We have as fellow-guests here W. M. James, Q.C., and his people, well known to us and agreeable. The Bishop of London has been here for a night, returning from the baths of St. Moritz, and one day Mrs. Horace Twiss sat next us at dinner, and had many inquiries after you. She now seems to spend a good deal of her time in foreign travel.

I have seen the famous falls of the Rhine at Schaffhausen and was disappointed. The hydraulic phenomenon is grand, the volume of water far exceeding anything of the sort in England—say, perhaps, as much as that of the Tees at Durham when full, or more, but the banks at the point are not beautiful, and the sight is spoilt by too much showmanship.  Above and below the falls the river is beautiful, but at the falls not so.  Above, the colour of the water was exceedingly blue, like nothing to be seen in the cold north.  We have had the great pleasure of an unexpected meeting with F——, who delayed his return for a couple of days in order to see us.  There is a Russian lady here with a trunk five feet long, three feet wide and deep, weighing 800 pounds, and which four men can lift with difficulty.—Yours affectionately, W. F. P.

One day while at Berne we attended a Peace Congress, and sitting, as spectators only, in a gallery heard the most furious and warlike denunciations made—"Bientôt se lévera le soleil glorieux de la paix, et puis a tout despote, a tout tyran, guerre à outrance, gue-r-r-re à mort," and so forth, of which we soon had enough, but had a franc's worth of amusement each in return for our admission money.  From Berne we visited Fribourg, and wondered why it had never been selected as the scene of a melodrama.  With the old covered bridge, the forge, the suspension bridge, the river, the walls and towers, and the railway, there might be a magnificent display of scenery, with some tremendous effects. In Paris we saw some good plays and operas. At the Français there was *Paul Forestier*, with that excellent actress Favart, Delaunay, and Coquelin *ainé;* and on another evening, for a *lever du rideau, Iris,* followed by *Il ne faut jurer de rien,* with Got and Delaunay (in which Got's back is wonderful), and *La Bataille de Dames.* At the Opera we saw *L'Africaine,* and Ambroise Thomas's *Hamlet,* with Nillson as Ophelia, and Faure as Hamlet.

We dined very often at the Café Voisin, an excellent *restaurant.*

17*th October.*—To Fryston. In the house were the Duke of Wellington, Wentworth, and Somerset Beaumont, Edmund Oldfield, Richard Doyle, Moran, the United States Secretary of Legation, and others. During the visit we twice went into Leeds to see the Art Exhibition then going on there.

14*th November.*—At the Athenæum. Willes kindly promised to take one of my sons on circuit with him as Marshal. He afterwards took both F—— and W——, to their great advantage. The former learned a great deal of law from him, and conceived a deep regard and respect for him personally, which he has never failed to evince on all suitable occasions, having lately (1887) dedicated to his memory his *Treatise on the Law of Torts*, rightly describing him as "a man courteous and accomplished, a judge wise and valiant." The premature death of Willes was a great loss to the judicial bench and to his friends.

*2d December.*—Tyndall showed me in the laboratory of the Royal Institution the polarisation of light by the particles (90 per cent organic germs) floating in the air.

*11th January* 1869.— I dined with H. Merivales. Marquis of Lorne, Froudes, Benjamin Moran (U.S. Sec. Leg.), Sir Louis and Lady Malet, Mrs. Gray, Frederic Harrison.

*15th January.*—Took Augusta Ritchie to hear Tyndall at the Royal Institution. In his lecture he gave a theory accounting for the blue light of the sky. A day or two afterwards the following couplet was sent to him :—

"*Dialogue between Urania, the Mother of the Heavens, and Celestine, the Nymph of the Blue Sky.*

*Urania.* Tell me, sweet Celestine, what makes you pout ?
*Celestine.* O! mother dear ! *that* Tyndall's found me out."

HATTON, 16*th January* 1869.

MY DEAR FRED—Mrs. Somerville[1] is indeed most interesting, and especially in the first volume from p. 90 to p. 150, where she does extract something like law and order. I had thought the spectrum one of the most promising and interesting subjects that could excite and reward a searcher after physical truths, but it appeared to me that every rule was so eaten up by exceptions, and every change of pressure, temperature, and light brought so many changes and varieties of result, that one might as well go to a heap of brickbats and endeavour to arrange them in classes, orders, genera, and species. . . . I begin to think that the result of chemical investigation cannot be reduced to a perfect system, any more than the vegetable and animal forms can be arranged in a perfect set of divisions of any sort.—Yours affectionately,

F. POLLOCK.

The last remark in the above letter has been much confirmed by the recent researches and speculations of Lockyer, Crookes, and Nordenskiöld upon the constitution of the supposed chemical elements of matter. Some day it will probably be proved that they have all been evolved from a common origin, just as the existing species of organic life have been traced by Darwin to a common ancestry.

23*d January* 1869.

MY DEAR FRED—Peel, I have no doubt, made a remark

---

[1] *On the Physical Sciences.*

such as Pemberton[1] records, but my recollection of the facts is this. The dispute between Denman (Chief Justice) and the House of Commons arose between Peel's first and second administration. We returned to office in September 1841. Follett and I had separately (without any communication with each other) come to the same conclusion, which was not one of principle but of practice, viz. that Denman was quite wrong, but that the mode of asserting the right of the Commons was not by committing attorneys' clerks who served process, or attorneys themselves who ordered writs to be issued, or even the plaintiffs themselves, but by plea and appeal to a Court of Error, which ultimately would go to the High Court of Parliament, commonly called *The Lords*, but in reality both Houses (though the Commons never attend, as the lay Lords now do not), and right would be done. Peel most handsomely in public said he was bound by the opinion of his law-officers and must surrender his own. Wilde, late Attorney-General, was furious for committing everybody; he was Pym, Follett and I were two Hampdens; a majority approved of our moderation. Peel was very selfish; he did not stick to his friends as Castlereagh and Palmerston did. Frank Bonham got into a sort of scrape about taking some shares in a Company. Peel would not speak for him; I think he did not even vote. I and Follett spoke—certainly I did—and the motion against Bonham was negatived. But who reviewed an unpublished book? Surely it was wrong; you might as well review a private letter if a few copies were printed for the use of the family. . . . When I was first appointed Attorney-General, the Solicitor-Generalship was

---

[1] In the *Memoirs of Lord Kingsdown* (T. Pemberton-Leigh), privately printed, and reviewed in the *Edinburgh Review*.

offered to Pemberton before Follett; he declined it, it was generally understood because it could not last. Follett accepted it. Neither P. nor F. were Q.C.'s, and F. not in Parliament.—Yours affectionately, F. P.

*24th January.*—Brookfield came to lunch, and told us how he had enlivened his colleagues on a recent occasion, when he was present as an Honorary Canon at a Chapter held in St. Paul's to receive the *Congé d'élire* for Jackson as Bishop of London. There was a printed programme of the proceedings, and it was stated that members of the Chapter cited to attend would be held contumacious, without adding "if they did not appear." Some of the clergy attempted to defend the omission by reference to preceding words. Brookfield stood up and protested against it. He was a poor man, he said, and could not afford to be contumacious. Such mistakes were very serious; but such things did sometimes occur, and it reminded him of a notice he had seen outside a poulterer's shop in the Borough: "A lot of live Ostend rabbits on sale. Any person wishing to buy one will be skinned and trussed, ready for roasting in five minutes." The assembled divines had listened with gravity to this speech, which was very seriously delivered, and sat silent for half a minute after it was ended, and then broke into peals of laughter—a merriment of parsons such as Dr. Johnson would have disapproved.

59 Montagu Square, W.,<br>
24<i>th January</i> 1869.</div>

My dear Father—The writer of the notice of Lord Kingsdown's *Reminiscences* in the *Edinburgh Review* is Henry Reeve, the editor of the *Review*, who was the person to whom the Pemberton family entrusted the memoirs for private publication—if one may use such a contradictory expression. I made Reeve's acquaintance many years ago dining at Thackeray's, when he lived in Great Coram Street. I see a review of Campbell's two posthumous lives (Lyndhurst and Brougham) announced to appear in the forthcoming *Quarterly*, but the book itself is not yet out. I wonder whether any life of Campbell by Brougham is left among the latter lord's papers.

I shall have a notice of Dean Milman's *Annals of St. Paul's* in the next number of *Fraser*, which I will send you, as I fancy you have not got the book itself. If you had the book it would be superfluous to read the review, which is entirely drawn from it.

We dined yesterday at Grove's—I should think one of the first occasions of their giving a dinner since the great calamity in their family. We met Sir Henry Holland, and F—— and I are to breakfast with him to-morrow. He was great about Campbell, whom he knew well.—Yours affectionately, W. F. P.

59 MONTAGU SQUARE, W.,
*28th January* 1869.

MY DEAR FATHER—I have got Campbell's posthumous volume, but have only looked through it. Hayward's review in the *Quarterly* deals severely with it, as it seems to deserve. With all Campbell's bad taste, the *Life of Lyndhurst* contains passages hardly to be expected even from him, and one is surprised that they should have been suffered to go forth. There is just published a collection of biographical notices by Miss Martineau, collected from the newspapers in which they appeared—short and not always accurate, but shrewd and amusing, and generally well-informed. The three chancellors—Brougham, Lyndhurst, and Campbell—cut an equally bad figure. Last night we went to drink tea with Carlyle at Chelsea. He has returned pretty much to his old self, but was quiet and subdued. Tyndall dined and went with us. Froude was there. It might have been better to have had Carlyle alone.—Yours affectionately, W. F. P.

*9th February.*—Dined at Fishmongers' Hall with James Spicer, my friend and colleague in the Direction at the Equitable Life Office. It was a dinner conceived by Mr. Moore, the Master of the Company, a well-known philanthropist, to bring together some distinguished members of the Church of England and some eminent Nonconformist ministers. Accordingly there were present the Archbishop of York, and the bishops of London, Oxford, and Peterborough, the last of whom made a most amusing speech. The Dissenters were represented by Binney, Brock, and others, who seemed to enjoy it, but did not quite know how to take it in the speeches made by them after dinner.

*15th February.*—Dined with Spicer at his country-house at Woodford. Sat next to Sir George Cartier, for whose head a reward had been offered after the Canadian rebellion of 1837, and who afterwards became a most loyal minister of the Crown in the colony of Canada. He could not easily speak English, and his French was old-fashioned and slowly spoken. He said there was no original French literature in Canada except for the purposes of journalism, as they got their books from France. But he contended that Canadian French was better than that now current in Paris, and that it was the true representative of the Augustan age of French literature in the time of Louis XIV. This was the only occasion on which I ever talked with a man still wearing his head on his shoulders, but which he had once been in great danger of losing.

59 Montagu Square,<br>*27th February* 1870.

My dear Father—You will receive in a day or two

by book post three magazines for March—*St. Paul's, Macmillan, Fraser.* This is a remarkable conjunction in the literary firmament. These three magazines each contain an article from this house. J—— has one in *St. Paul's* on Miss Austen and her novels, prompted by the recent life of her, and another in *Macmillan* entitled "The French Stage." In *Fraser* there is a paper of mine in review of Faraday's life, which, if you have not read the book itself, may help to give you a notion of it.—Yours affectionately,
W. F. P.

*7th March.*—Dined Simeon's. Lord Chancellor O'Hagan, Monsells, Lecky.

*16th March.*—To reading by Dickens at St. James's Hall. He gave Boots at the Holly Tree, the scene between Bill Sykes and Nancy, and a bit of Mrs. Gamp. What an actor he would have made! what a success he must have had if he had gone to the bar! His power of reproducing a scene and bringing to the very eyes of his audience its exact features and the relative bearings of its composing parts has never been equalled. This would have been an invaluable quality in many cases at the bar. He could always at a glance take in the contents and furniture of a room, and in this way was able to astonish his friends by performing some of the feats made famous by Houdin the conjuror. In the scene on the steps of London Bridge from *Oliver Twist* the whole arrangement of the locality, and the positions of the speakers and listeners, stood out in a kind of reality when accentuated by the voice and gestures of Dickens.

*20th March.*—At breakfast Charles Eliot Norton, of Cambridge, Mass., U.S., and Aubrey de Vere. Norton gave me his translation of the *Vita Nuova*.

*31st March.*—At dinner Mr. and Mrs. C. Eliot Norton, Aubrey de Vere, the De Mussys, Mrs. Brookfield, Oldfield, Froude, Lecky.

*3d April.*—Breakfast Club at Sir John Lefevre's in Spring Gardens. Dufferin, Bruce (Home Secretary), Grant Duff, Simeon, Erskine May, Arthur Russell, Froude. It was said that the Irish in England were arming themselves with revolvers, and that depôts of arms were being formed in many towns. Subscriptions to buy arms were made under the guise of collections for the families of the Fenian prisoners. "General" O'Neill, their best man, was set aside for less able but more noisy leaders. Feuds between "Hibernians" and Fenians. The expedition against Canada from the United States abandoned for this year. Many rifles converted into breech-loaders in America to be sent over to Ireland. The proceedings at Cabinet Councils were described. The Lord President nominally presided, and would take the divisions, if any. Gladstone sits in centre of table. Foreign affairs always come first. There is no record of what takes place, but the Premier always writes to the Queen an account of each council. No one is admitted to the room, but the junior Cabinet minister goes to the door if anything arrives— Goschen now does this. The likeness of Lord Granville in *Vanity Fair* arrived in an official-looking envelope directed to him, and was delivered to him in Cabinet. It was handed round, and for some moments suspended a discussion on the Irish Church. Lord Granville liked it well enough to order fifty copies. Erskine May mentioned that he had seen a note-book of the proceedings of Cabinet Councils kept by Lord Sydenham (Poulett Thompson), now in the possession of Poulett Scrope. It was very curious and interesting, often giving the exact words used by Lord Grey and other ministers.

Bright is said to be doing and acting his new part of Cabinet minister well, is proud of his black velvet suit (worn without a sword), and looks well in it. He is much in request by great ladies, and told some one who asked him when he was going to speak in the late Irish Church debate, "I have arranged with the Princess Louise to rise at half-past ten."

In the afternoon talked with Browning at the Athenæum about *The Ring and the Book*. He said that he had at last secured the ear of the public, but that he had done it by vigorously assaulting it, and by telling his story four times over. He added that he had perhaps after all failed in making himself intelligible, and said it was like bawling into a deaf man's trumpet, and then being asked not to speak so loud, but more distinctly.

*14th April.*—A reading at 59 Montagu Square, in which Mrs. Stirling and Brookfield were so kind as to take part. We had scenes from *Much Ado about Nothing*, the story of Lefevre, beautifully given by Brookfield, and Tennyson's "Poet's Song." Some fifty people came.

*15th April.*—As one of the Masters of the Court of Exchequer I attended the House of Lords to take up the roll of proceedings in a suit taken up in Error to the House of Lords. This duty used formerly to be performed by one of the Judges. It was an absurd business. One had to make the usual three low bows in approaching the bar of the House. Then one was sworn to answer truly all questions, and the Chancellor asked, "What have you got there?" To which reply had to be made, "The roll in a cause of Smith against Jones brought in Error before your Lordships." Then one was asked if it was in the same state as when received, which was a proper question to a person bringing anything from abroad, but not applicable when an official of the Court was producing a document of which he was supposed to have the custody, although, in point of fact, the roll was not completed until it was wanted, and was put into the Master's hand only a minute or two before he handed it in to the Clerk of the Parliament, who came down to the bar to administer the oath and take possession of the roll. All this was very sensibly abolished by the Appellate Judicature Act of

1876. On this occasion I witnessed the quaint ceremony of introducing a new peer (in the person of Lord Lawrence), which is so curiously travestied, although with considerable adherence to what actually takes place, by Victor Hugo in *L'homme qui rit*. I must have performed this function several times during my tenure of the office of Master, and was always reminded by it of the story of Lyndhurst and W. Holmes. It was told as having happened soon after Lyndhurst was made a peer, and was known to be lamenting that he had no son to succeed him, and at a time when the Lord Chancellor used to leave the woolsack and come down in person to the bar to receive every bill brought up from the House of Commons, for which he had a fee of five guineas. Upon one occasion Holmes had charge of the Bills from the Commons, and had to answer the question, "What have you got there?" many times, always giving the title of the Bill. At last the journeys from the woolsack to the bar and back again grew rather wearisome, and Holmes enlivened the monotony of the proceedings by answering the "What have you got there?" by saying

"A bill to enable your Lordship to beget male heirs."—"You be d—d!" said the Chancellor, and regained his seat.

*8th May.*—At breakfast at Lacaita's. He showed a book of impressions of seals which had belonged to Voltaire. It was like a quarto copy book, and contained a great number of seals torn from letters with the names of their owners written underneath. When he received letters he used to compare the seals with those in the book to ascertain from whom the letters came, and unless he liked their writers he did not open the letters.

*13th May.*—Dined at Donne's. He had been at the Archbishop of Dublin's the day before and met the Bishop of Oxford, who was in great force, and telling stories in a way rather to frighten Mrs. Trench. One was of the contributions of a housemaid, accustomed to live in high ecclesiastical places, to a knowledge of the personal habits of her successive employers. "The work is very different, particular in filling and emptying of baths. Now the Bishop of Oxford (Wilberforce), he have his bath regular every day. The Archbishop of Canterbury (Tait), he have his bath every day except Sundays; but the Dean of Westminster (Stanley) he never use only a wet towel."

CAMBRIDGE, 18*th May* 1869.

MY DEAR FATHER—You may like to have an account of the impression made on me by the Macaulay statue in Trinity College Chapel, written from the spot, and I accordingly avail myself of the writing facilities at the Union for that purpose. The statue looks extremely well, and is placed half way between the door and the screen. The light falls well upon it, and it is praised by every one. It is at present one of three sitting figures, and when Whewell is added, also to be executed by Woolner, and also to be sessile, it will be one of four—enough to draw together at night, when not under observation, for a game at whist, with Newton to look on and calculate the chances of the odd trick, unless, indeed, they are less peacefully employed, and Bacon endeavours to revenge himself on Macaulay for his scurvy treatment of him in the *Edinburgh Review*. We are going through a very agreeable series of hospitalities, to terminate this afternoon, when we return to town. W—— is well, and reading as much as he can; a great favourite with every one. I hope you are quite strong again.—Yours affectionately, W. F. P.

*23d May.*—Moulton to lunch, and took him to see Babbage and his workshops.

*16th June.*—C. C. S. dinner at Richmond—Vernon Lushington in chair.

*21st June.*—Public meeting at the Royal Institution to promote subscriptions for a memorial to Faraday, with the Prince of Wales in the chair. Dumas, the chemist, was present and made a speech in French. The memorial ultimately took the form of a marble statue, designed and partially executed by Foley, and completed after his death by his pupil Brock. It was intended for Westminster Abbey, and Dean Stanley had selected for it almost the only available space. But the religious scruples of his widow and of Faraday's family would not allow it to be placed either in the Abbey or in St. Paul's, on the ground that he would not have entered in his lifetime a place of worship other than one belonging to his own peculiar denomination. In fact, Faraday did decline to attend the public funeral of the Duke of Wellington, because he was buried in St. Paul's Cathedral. The statue now stands very appropriately in the hall of the Royal Institution, where Faraday's work was done, and in whose service he spent the greater part of his life.

*26th June.*—Came to breakfast W. C. Cartwright, J. W. Clark, Herbert Spencer, Currey, Holtzmann, F. Garden, Aubrey de Vere.

*10th July.*—To breakfast, Venables, Mr.

and Mrs. Cornish, S. Laurence, Kinglake, F. W. Gibbs, Deutsch.

*12th July.*—Dined with Frederick Locker in Victoria Street, to meet Tennyson, just returned from a tour in Switzerland with him.

# CHAPTER VII

### CAEN—ST. LO

IN the autumn of 1869 we were in France again, going by Newhaven, Dieppe, Rouen, and Caen, to Avranches. At Caen one saw the churches and other sights. As the central town of an agricultural district, it reminded me of Ipswich, with its similar shops and narrow streets, but the streets were as noisy and crowded as Cheapside. At the theatre Dejazet (æt. 72) was acting her old part in *Les Trois Gamins*, rather a sad sight, as she only acts, poor woman, because she would otherwise starve. She did not, however, create much attraction, and the house was only half full. The railway to Avranches was not completed farther than to St. Lo, where we had to spend some time, and I found the butter market very amusing. The butter seemed chiefly intended for the English market, and was sold by English weight. We went on to Avranches by a *diligence*, of which my wife, my son W——, and myself occupied the *coupé* immediately behind the driver, and heard all the talk and gossip of the road. At one place the driver was to have left a parcel for a notary, which contained the printed placards of a sale of land, the due circulation and posting of which is, by French law, necessary to the validity of the transaction. It was therefore rather an important parcel, and the driver took it with much care out of the box on which he sat and placed it beside him, conveniently for delivering, a little while before he came to the notary's house. When he looked for it, it was gone, and must have fallen off the seat. He had to alight to announce the loss, about which he talked all the rest of the way, thinking of all the harm that might happen to him in consequence, and chiefly fearing the vengeance of the notary, " I'l pourrait bien me faire perdre quelque belle succession." Avranches disappointed us. There is a magnificent view, in which the chief object is Mont St. Michel, but the town itself is mean and uninteresting.

Here W—— became so unwell as to require medical advice, and his mother went in person to secure a doctor. On her way back to the hotel she lost her watch with its appendages, and, after consulting our landlord, orders were given to the public crier or *tambour* to offer a reward for the recovery of the watch. Every one in the house immediately became interested in the matter, and the most sympathetic expressions were used. We went to sit in the garden of the hotel, and presently heard the crier going round the town, beating his drum and making proclamation, sometimes nearer and sometimes farther off. At the end of an hour or two we were aware of a stir and a sound of voices crying "C'est trouvé, c'est trouvé." A little procession entered the garden, with *tambour* at the head of it—three prettily dressed girls, one of whom had found the watch, and a following of the hotel servants and idlers from the town. It was Sunday; all were decked in their best, and under the trees in the garden it was like a scene in a ballet. *Tambour* explained how the watch had been seen and picked up by one of the girls— farmer's daughters from the neighbourhood—as she was coming out of church. The watch was restored, to the delight of the "*assistance*," and the finder received a half napoleon, which was evidently more than had been expected, for the remark went round, "*C'est un dot pour elle*," and some wishes were expressed that an English lady would again lose her watch and have it found with a similar result. At Avranches we fell in with Anthony Trollope and his wife, whom we joined again in a day or two at St. Malo. My eldest son came to us at Avranches, and with him and the present Master of Caius College, Cambridge, and his wife, I went to Mont St. Michel—a very wonderful and beautiful thing. The bridge was not then built which permanently connects the island with the mainland, and we made our way to it on foot, struggling against a boisterous wind along a narrow stone causeway which was practicable long before the sands were sufficiently uncovered by the falling tide to allow of our carriage's crossing them. We had for a guide a most picturesque-looking fellow, with a bronze skin and some floating drapery, which made him look like a figure from a picture by Nic. Poussin. He had been in the French cavalry, and was full of stories of his prowess in battle, and in saving lives from shipwreck since he had been living at Mont St. Michel, which seemed mostly lies, but which he thought would go down with his "*monde*," as he called us. In returning, there was a pool of water to be crossed to get to the carriage. He caught up Mrs. Ferrers, as Nessus might have laid hold of Deianira, and I followed in humble pick-a-back, like Æneas on the shoulders of Anchises. Ferrers and F—— were too proud for this, and went round the pool. In driving back to Avranches there was an adventure with a couple of men in charge of a timber wain. The road was narrow, and they were very surly in making room for us to pass, and gave our carriage so little room that one of our wheels touched one of their horses, but did no harm, upon which there was a storm of *sacrés* and so forth. Presently afterwards our driver took a wrong turn, and when we regained the right road there were our friends with the timber wain before us again, and resolutely refusing to let us pass. If we had been in England, as we were three men to two, we might have used our *vis major* and forced a passage, but in a foreign country this might have got us into trouble, and for some minutes we had to follow the wain at a walking pace. Then, after taking a good look at the men, I commenced a parley. The elder man was a sullen-looking, oldish man, and I saw no chance of success with him, but appealed to the gallantry of the younger one. I pointed out that he was keeping a lady from her dinner, and punishing us all for the fault of our driver, who was a countryman of his own, and was not our servant. I might have quoted to him the case of Laugher *v.* Pointer, as to the legal immunity of the hirer of a carriage from the consequences of an accident due to the negligence of the driver when he is a servant of the owner of the vehicle, but thought it would be thrown away upon him. But after a little coaxing and flattery of the chivalry of the French nation, of which in truth they really have mighty little, in regard to women, I moved the young man to go and speak to the other, and, with much reluctance, they made way, allowed our carriage to pass, and we reached the hotel at Avranches in good time for dinner. Spending a night at

Le Mans, then untouched by the horrors of war, we made for Paris, where, for the first time, we descended at the excellent little Hotel S. Romain, Rue du Dauphin, since incorporated into the Rue S. Roche, where the good host, M. Bélard, and his wife made us extremely comfortable, as they have done on many subsequent occasions. There was a good deal of play-going. We saw the charming Gallimarié in *La Petite Fadette*, and *Diane de Lys* with the incomparable Desclée, at the Gymnase. At the Français we saw the *Menteur*, with Delaunay and Got, preceded by a perfect recitation of Musset's *Nuit d'Octobre* given by Favart and Delaunay; and on another night *Julie*, preceded by *Le Cheveu Blanc*, and followed by *Le Dernier Quartier*, with Favart (an actress whose fame has been rather unjustly eclipsed by that of some of her successors), Lafontaine, Reichemberg, and Febvre. On the last occasion a thing happened which would always prevent me from feeling certain in a case of identity, unless I had actually spoken with the person in question. We were sitting on the side of the house in the front row of the *balcon*, when I noticed, as I thought, Sir James

Hannen in a similar place exactly opposite to us. I mentioned it to my wife and sons, and said I would go round to speak to him at the end of the act. I did so, but his seat was vacant, and I went to look for him in the *foyer*, and then, as the bell was ringing for the next act, I went to the door behind his seat and, as I thought, saw him returned to his place again. I looked for him as we were leaving the theatre, to no purpose. Two or three days afterwards I met Hannen in London and mentioned I had seen him at the Français, and we discussed the play of *Julie*, which I fancied we had seen together. I mentioned the piece which had preceded it, and he said, "No, it was not that;" and for a moment or two we could not make out our disagreement. Then he named the date of his seeing *Julie*, and it turned out that it was a day or two before that on which we had seen it, and that he had left Paris before the day on which I was so positive that I had seen him at the theatre. It would have been a very good anecdote to tell to a jury in a defence turning upon a supposed mistake of identity. In returning to London we were fortunate in having the company of Tyndall, and of Professor

Flower and his wife. An enjoyable visit to
Venables at his beautiful place of Llysdinam,
on the Wye, brought the long vacation to its
close.

59 MONTAGU SQUARE,<br>
8th December 1869.

MY DEAR FATHER—De la Pryme has sent me a cheque for £60 odd, the balance of the Macaulay statue fund, which I have paid over to the Literary Fund, according to desire, as one of its treasurers. We shall have a Committee meeting this afternoon, when a formal vote of thanks will be passed and duly transmitted to Sir Charles Trevelyan, to De la Pryme (who should, I think, be included), and yourself.

I was on Saturday and Sunday on a visit to Tennyson at his new house on the ridge of Blackdown, near Haslemere—a fine situation, occupied by a handsome and commodious house just built for him by James Knowles. He read me some of his forthcoming new poems. Yesterday I dined in company with twenty people, a great crowd and no company, and such an assemblage of big-wiggery. Two Chiefs, a Lord Justice, a Vice-Chancellor, a Baron, the Solicitor-General, an ex-Attorney-General, an honourable Q.C., and an honourable utter barrister, a Chief Commissioner, a surgical baronet, an Under-Secretary of State, the editor of the *Edinburgh Review*, and a marshal at each end of the table. But I had a pleasant enough *tête-à-tête* with one of my next neighbours.—Yours affectionately, W. F. P.

*18th December.*—To Bedgebury Park, on visit to Beresford Hopes. Found there Lady

Rolle, Cardwells, Gathorne Hardys, Sir E. Cust, Venables, etc. We were driven to the house from the station in one of Beresford Hope's carriages, which had been taking to it some departing guests, and so passed the lodge of the Park without anything occurring to attract attention. But the next day Sir E. Cust asked me if I did not think it odd that a toll should be taken from carriages entering the Park, and one learned that a road lay across it which saved going a long way round, and that this was a great convenience to the neighbourhood. And as the traffic made the repair of the road, which is of some length, an expensive affair, it seemed fair that the people who got the benefit of it should contribute to its maintenance. Carriages bringing visitors to the house were not exempted from paying toll, because it would be so easy for unscrupulous persons to say at the lodges that they were going to the house.

*13th* and *14th January* 1870.—Performances in Montagu Square of *Weather Permitting*, taken from the French *La Pluie et le Beau Temps*, and *Madame Celestine*, an original piece, in both of which my wife took part as Mrs. Wilfred Montagu. F—— was in the bill as

Mr. F. Le Jeune, and W—— as Mr. Walter Montagu. M—— Emilius made his first appearance as Miss Emily Montagu in a female part. Edith Richmond kindly helped us, appearing in the bills as Miss Edith Sheen.

*12th February.*—Dined with Montagu Smith at Grosvenor Gate. Lord Chelmsford, Chief Justice Cockburn, Baron Pigot, Loftus Wigram, Karslake, Gifford, Edward Romilly, C. Baron Kelly, F. W. Gibbs, Montagu Bere, R. Burke.

*22d February.*—Dinner at home. Lord Houghton, Master of Trinity, W. C. Cartwright, G. S. Venables, Brookfield, Froude.

*15th March.*—Dined Benzon's (Kensington Palace Gardens). Motleys, De Mussys, Browning, Leighton, Cartwright, etc.

*3d April.*—Was elected a member of the Dilettanti Society. This Society was founded early in the last century, and has counted among its members many eminent statesmen, wits, men of letters and of fashion. Charles James Fox and George Selwyn belonged to it. Sir Joseph Banks became its secretary in the same year as that in which he was elected President of the Royal Society, and held both offices together for nearly twenty years. Sir Thomas Lawrence was at one time secretary, and so was Mr. W. R. Hamilton for thirty years. My immediate predecessor as secretary (as I afterwards became) was Sir Edward Ryan, the eminent Indian judge. Originally the qualification for membership was that the candidate had been met in Italy by the proposing member. Upon one occasion, however, a candidate was elected who had been met at Avignon—a place at the time certainly more Italian than French in its associations. When the mistake was discovered, in order to make the election valid a special resolution was passed "that, in the opinion of the Society, Avignon is in Italy." But in order to prevent the establishment of a dangerous precedent, a second resolution was carried "that, in the opinion of this Society, Avignon is the only town in France which is in Italy." On the serious and important work done and doing by the Society of Dilettanti in the encouragement of the knowledge of Greek and Roman art it is unnecessary to dwell, as it is so well known from the numerous publications published under the auspices and at the expense of the Society.

*7th April.*—Concert at 5 Hyde Park Place, where Dickens was then living; Joachim, C. Halle, Santley. This was the first return of Dickens to general society after his separation from Mrs. Dickens.

*12th April.*—At dinner Baron and Lady Martin, Douglas Freshfields, Benzons, Anthony Trollopes, Browning, Lecky, Valentia Donne.

*23d April.*—My cousin George, the eminent surgeon, extracted a particle of grit from my left eye. The instinctive action of the eye to protect itself was too strong to allow of my remaining sufficiently quiet for this very trifling operation, and I had to take chloroform. It was like rushing into a railway tunnel to the beats of a locomotive engine. During the few moments of semi-consciousness which preceded the return to ordinary existence, I seemed to myself to have composed some great poem—the subject of which was, however, never known to me.

*27th April.*—Laurence Oliphant, just returned from the United States, dined with us. He was full of the universal corruption prevailing in America—political, judicial, and commercial.

*1st May.*—Dined with the Dilettanti Society, and was admitted a member with all the quaint and curious solemnities which are practised on such occasions by the oldest surviving institution of its kind in London.

*7th May.*—Came to breakfast Lord Edmond Fitzmaurice, Cartwright, Venables, Hutton (of the *Spectator*), Sidney Colvin, S. Laurence, Spedding.

*20th May.*—Dined De Mussys. Afterwards to the Motleys, who have got Lord Yarborough's fine house in Arlington Street.

*28th May.*—To French play at Princess's Theatre; saw *Un Caprice* and *La Joi fait Peur*, in which Regnier was so great as the old servant. The only other performer of note was Madeleine Brohan. A few nights afterwards we saw them in *Les Demoiselles de S. Cyr.*

*8th June.*—C. C. S. dinner at Richmond—Helps president. Clifford staying with us, and went with me. Clifford was one of the most remarkable men of his time; his intellectual powers were prodigious; in the highest regions of mathematical science he had done much, and would have certainly done more in extending its powers and resources if his life had been prolonged. Whatever he did was done with ease and perfect mastery. He seemed to play with the infinite, and in the general relations of life the same ease and a pervading brilliancy existed. He had the rare quality of wit, and the still rarer one in England, of gaiety. His whole soul was full of love. He had few, if any, personal dislikes, but had very marked intellectual antipathies, to which he sometimes too much gave way. He was a daring and accomplished athlete in the gymnasium and a good dancer, always ready to turn from more serious occupation to fun and frolic. A friend once called him "an inspired kitten," and the name was at once adopted by many of his intimates.

*6th July.*—Dine John Walters, Upper Grosvenor Street. Met Lord and Lady A. Churchill, Lord and Lady Cairns, Cardwells, W. E. Forsters, Sir J. Hope Grant, Sir Frederick and Lady Rogers.

*7th July.*—Drury Lane Opera—*Otello* with Nielson, Mongini, Faure, Gardoni.

*9th July.*—Came to breakfast E. Twisleton, Kinglake, Townsend (of the *Spectator*), Deutsch, George Darwin, Watkiss Lloyd.

*15th July.*—With Houghton from the Athenæum to the House of Lords, and heard Lord Granville make the announcement of war between France and Prussia. The universal expectation was that in a fortnight the French would be at Frankfort, and would, for some time to come at least, have the best of it; and that it would be long before the Germans could take the field in great force.

*22d July.*—My father died at Hatton, aged 86 years and 11 months. In returning from the funeral in Hanworth churchyard I was in the same coach with my uncle Sir George Pollock (the Field-Marshal), and my uncle Mr. John Pollock, himself a very old man. In one of the obituary notices of my father which had appeared in the newspapers he was designated as the son of "a flourishing saddler" at Charing Cross. Now, I knew that he had been unable to keep my father at Cambridge, and that he owed his continued residence at the University to the generous kindness of Tavel, his tutor at Trinity College. I asked my uncle if his father had at any time been in good circumstances. He said yes; that he had the business of the King, the Prince of Wales, and the Royal Family, and that of the East India Company, and of some cavalry regiments. His connection with the Royal Family was unfortunate for him. When the Prince of Wales's debts were paid by the nation on his marriage, he owed him £3000. In discharging these debts large reductions were made, and no interest was allowed. Some tradesmen's bills were cut down by fifty or sixty per cent. Ten per cent only was struck off my grandfather's bill, and the persons who attended to the matter told him that they were sorry to have to do this, as his charges were perfectly fair and honest, but that they must take off something in conformity with their general instructions.

*2d November.*—Dined with Lord Vernon, to meet Mr. and Mrs. Parsons of Boston (he a translator of Dante), Lacaita, the William Vernons, and Professor Pierce, a distinguished American mathematician.

*10th November.*—Evening with Carlyle at Chelsea. Talking of the Franco-German war, he called Napoleon the Third a copper captain, who was breaking his addled goose's egg against a rock of adamant.

*23d November.*—Dined Lord Justice James.

Met Madame Mohl, who came to breakfast with us three days afterwards.

*10th December.*—Dined with James Knowles at Clapham. Tennyson was there, and read to us the sermon from " Aylmer's Field."

Epigram upon the Declaration of Papal Infallibility at the Œcumenical Council in 1870 :

> " Quando Eva morse, e morder fece il pomo,
> Iddio per salvar l'uomo, si fece uomo ;
> Ma il Vicario di Christo, Pio Nono,
> Per far uomo schiavo, si fece Dio."

*31st January* 1871.—At dinner Clifford Harrison. He read Tennyson's " Brook" and " Locksley Hall."

*7th March.*—Reading at home by Lady Pollock and Clifford Harrison, and Megan Watts singing.

*18th March.*—Elected to the Cosmopolitan Club.

*12th April.* — Performance of *Travellers' Tales*, adapted from Octave Feuillet's *Le Village*, and *Lady Vivian at Home*, in which that remarkable and delightful person Alice L'Estrange (afterwards Mrs. Laurence Oliphant) took part.

*5th May.*—To the Opera Comique Theatre

in the Strand, where the members of the Comédie Française, driven from Paris by the siege, were now performing on their own venture. The piece was *Il ne faut jurer de rien*, in which Got and Delaunay are seen at their best. It was some time before people in London got to know what they could now see —the best French plays, with all the parts well filled; for only a few of the company came over, and these were the most distinguished, such as Bressant, Coquelin, and Favart, along with those already mentioned. At first the theatre was very moderately filled, but by the end of their time it was always crowded.

The French company came to London on their own account, knowing nothing of English theatres, and unable to speak English. Delaunay, with Thiron and others, was in lodgings in one of the small streets running out of the Strand. One day they wanted some eggs, but were unable to make the servant maid of the house understand their wishes. They tried drawing ovals in the air with their fingers, and other signs, without effect. At last Thiron began to crow like a cock and to flap his arms like wings, in which the others imitated him;

then the mind of the damsel was opened, and in a few minutes a dish of the desired eggs was produced. It was very amusing to hear Delaunay, when we came to know him afterwards, describe how "*cette pauvresse*" was finally made to understand what was wanted.

21*st May.*—Dean Stanley's funeral sermon on Sir John Herschel, buried in the Abbey on the preceding Friday.

22*d May.*—*L'Aventurière,* with Favart, Bressant, and Coquelin, by the Comédie Française. This was the day on which the army of Versailles entered Paris to put down the frightful insurrection of the Commune. On the 24th the Tuileries were burnt, and the Theatre Français was in the greatest danger of being consumed.

8*th June.*—*Un Cas de Conscience, Mercadet.*

10*th June.*—Dined with Charles at Putney, and afterwards to Madame Viardot.

14*th June.*—C. C. S. dinner at Richmond—Tom Taylor presided.

15*th June.*—*Barbière de Seville*—Bressant, Coquelin, Talbot.

24*th June.*—Breakfast with Henry Cowper, at his brother's house, 4 St. James's Square, in a large dining-room on first floor, looking into a garden at the back of the house, and hung with Vandyke portraits. Lord Dufferin said that the young American ladies in London were complaining of want of attention to them in English gentlemen. "They don't *bunch* us," meaning that they are not presented with bouquets or bunches of flowers. He mentioned the threat of a girl who had been jilted, " I'll breach him."

*1st July.*—At breakfast Roden Noel, Lewis Wingfield, G. F. Armstrong, James Knowles, Holtzmann, W. D. Christie.

*8th July.*—*Dejcûner* given to the actors of the Comédie Française at the Crystal Palace upon their leaving London to return to Paris, after their troubled and anxious but successful season in London. I was on the executive committee, which had been appointed at a meeting held at the Rolls House, on the invitation of Sir W. D. Hardy; but Lewis Wingfield, Joseph Knight, Alfred Thompson, and Mr. Cosens, who acted as treasurer, were the persons most concerned in securing the great success which crowned the affair. The breakfast was held in the then existing tropical department of the Crystal Palace, which was beautifully decorated, and it was an afternoon of bright sunshine for the subsequent adjournment outside for coffee. Lords Granville, Dufferin, Houghton, Powerscourt, and Townshend sent their carriages to bring down the guests by road, under the care of Wingfield and Leighton (not yet Sir Frederick), the latter of whom designed the invitation card, the original of which was afterwards given to the Comédie, and is now framed and kept among the treasures of the Theatre Français. No one but the invited guests was allowed to have a copy of this card. Dufferin was in the chair, and made a charming speech in French, proposing the health of the guests, ending with: "N'oublions pas que dans, ces migrations et ces excursions triomphales vous suivez l'exemple de l'initiateur du drame primitif en Grece.

"' Dicitur et plaustris vexisse poemata Thespis.'"

Got, the *doyen* of the company, returned thanks, and proposed the memory of Shakespeare, to which Alfred Wigan responded. Lord Granville followed in a very happy vein, commencing with "*Il ne faut jurer de rien*"—in allusion to his previous uncertainty whether he should be able to be present—and proposed the health of the Chairman, to which he replied in English. I had breakfasted in company with Dufferin in the morning at Lord Acton's, and went down with him to Sydenham. At the beginning I sat with other members of the committee in their allotted place, between Bancroft and Du Maurier, and with Louis Viardot opposite. Afterwards I was called up to take the place reserved for Lord Lytton, between Talbot and Delaunay, and had the pleasure of making an acquaintance with the latter, which improved into friendship in subsequent visits to Paris and when he came again to act in London. We went to Madame Viardot's in the evening.

*9th July.*—Afternoon at Little Holland House. Tennyson, Story, Mark Pattison, Sir H. Rawlinson, Watts, etc.

*16th July.*—To Tennysons at Aldworth, for a couple of nights.

*18th July.*—Dined De Mussys. Lord Justice James, Sir J. Colvile, Grove, Leighton, Viardot, Tourganieff.

*21st July.*—Afternoon party at W. Spottiswoode's in Grosvenor Place, to meet the Emperor of Brazil. His acquaintance with every one and everything was marvellous. The only mistake one heard of his making was in addressing Arthur Stanley as Dean of St. Paul's instead of Westminster. The social meetings at William Spottiswoode's house, whether in town or at Combe Bank, were always pleasant and well arranged. The scientific element was naturally represented in strength, but there was always a considerable infusion of literature, art, and fashion. Spottiswoode himself was a heart of gold—generous, affectionate, and devoted to his friends, and to the numbers of persons in his employment. A career full of performance and great further promise was too soon brought to a close, and no man's loss could have been more deeply lamented in the worlds of science and of business, and by his many attached friends.

*3d August.*—Visit to Wynne Finch's at Voelas, Llanrwst. We spent several weeks this autumn at Clovelly in the house of John Mills, fisherman and boat-builder, whose workshop on the way "down along" to Quay Pool was a sort of *succursale* to our lodgings in wet weather. There is nowhere a more singular and beautiful place than Clovelly—with its village hung in a steep ravine, like a glacier in a Swiss valley; with its little pier, surrounded by cliffs and woods; with the drive called the Hobby; and with the unique grounds of the "Court," full of the most varied kinds of sylvan scenery, and where within a distance of a few yards one may enjoy the finest sea prospects or the most charming inland views and immediate surroundings. The people in the village very friendly and simple, with a sprinkling among them of retired sea captains, whose conversations and the curiosities in their houses gave a sort of foreign flavour to the place. At this time the only inroads from the outer world used to be steamboat excursions once or twice a week from Ilfracombe or the Bristol Channel. The tourists would land, pass in wonder up the steep, narrow street, often making remarks as if their language was not one understood by the natives, and then rush back to their boat on the ringing of a bell. The landlord of the principal inn—also a farmer and boat-owner, and much interested in many kinds of knowledge—was a great character, and his wife's collection of old china, originally obtained from houses, cottages, etc., in the neighbourhood, was a remarkable one. The people were all much attached to their own village. One day on returning from seeing Westward Ho, I said to the driver, himself a bit of a character—a sort of Sam Weller in his way—that I was glad to get back to Clovelly. He replied, " I'm glad to hear you say so, sir. For my own part, I don't think anything of Westward Ho; I'd rather be hanged at Clovelly than live at Westward Ho."

*16th October.*—At Royal Institution, looking over catalogue of books with Vincent, the librarian, to ascertain what sets can be eliminated to make more space for additions, with the least injury to the library. It is often difficult enough to come to a satisfactory decision in such cases, as I have also found when sometimes similarly engaged when on the Library Committee at the Athenæum. After one has become thoroughly satisfied that a book or set of books may go, one is sure to be told by the librarian that they have been recently asked for, and then they have, of course, to be retained. A great many long sets of books were given to the London Library. Even old directories and court guides have their occasional value, and might furnish information not obtainable otherwise.

*2d November.*—Dined with Knowles at Clapham, to meet Tennyson.

*15th November.*—Dined W. Spottiswoode's. Lord Chancellor and Lady Hatherley, Goschens, George Brodrick, W. Longman, Bowens.

*23d November.* — Dined Henry Reeves. Froudes, Count Strzelecki, Sir Montagu Smith, Justice Keatinge.

*1st December.*—To Lyceum. H. Irving in *Bells*, and again on 18th.

*16th January* 1872. — Performance at 59 Montagu Square of *How will it End* and *My Aunt's Devices*. The first piece was adapted by J. W. Clark from *Un Cas de Conscience*, and the second was altered from *Les Projets de ma Tante* by Lady Pollock. The principal performers were my wife and W——, but in *How will it End*, as announced in the playbills, I made my first appearance for seven years, under the name of Mr. Lemaitre, in a small part in the first scene. J. W. Clark's dialogue was extremely good, and the piece was well acted by those to whom its success was due—a difficult thing to secure with a serious play in private theatricals.

*19th January.*—Mr. Evarts of New York came to breakfast. He is now in Europe to represent the United States Government before the arbitrators on the Alabama claims at Geneva. He is a spare man, looking about forty or forty-five years old, and in face a little like the first Napoleon. He has eleven children, which he said was not unusual. As a counsel he never has a fee of less than 250 dollars, or £50, for going into court. The ordinary fee to the leading counsel in an ordinary case equals £20, the junior being paid as an attorney. He said that he never took part in what is our attorneys' work, of getting up the case, and that he could refer to his instructions without knowing what was behind them in as much conscientious ignorance as a barrister does in England. His partners always collected the evidence, and otherwise got up the cases and drew the briefs. Sir Henry Holland afterwards told me that he believed Evarts makes ten or twelve thousand pounds a year ; and I gathered from himself that in the States all fees have to be earned by working for them. Cases are adjourned for the convenience of counsel, so that they can actually attend to them in person. There are not, as in England, any pickings of fees paid for which no work is done, briefs delivered, and fees paid, but not perhaps even opened or read, and so on.

*30th January.*—Dined Henry Taylors at East Sheen. Browning.

*1st February.*—Dined Sir Thomas Watson's. Lord Chancellor and Lady Hatherley, Sir T. Henry, Boxall, George Richmond, etc. An unfortunate clergyman, bearing the same name as our host, had been tried three weeks before at the Old Bailey and convicted of murdering his wife, but sentenced to confinement for life as a lunatic. He had used the Latin words, " Sæpe olim semper debere nocuit debitori," in an exculpatory statement written by him, and Sir T. Henry said that nothing had given Mr. Watson so much pain in the whole proceedings as having had his Latinity questioned. The Chancellor said that Lowe had divided the Cabinet upon it, and that he had voted in the majority affirming it to be good Latin. The Chancellor seemed very happy, notwithstanding the Collier affair, in which the course taken by the Government is almost universally condemned. Frank Doyle the other day said that the division of responsibility between the Chancellor and Mr. Gladstone in the recent appointment of Collier to the judgeship in the Privy Council, so as to make each individually innocent, reminded him of Sterne's story of the Abbess of Andouillet and the novice when dividing between them the pronunciation of the naughty words used to make the obstinate mule get on.

*2d February.*—To Cambridge with F—— for Commemoration Day dinner at Trinity. Airy, the Astronomer Royal, spoke at immense length in returning thanks on his health being given, and some one remarked that *Greenwich* time was more like eternity.

*15th February.*— Dined at Fishmongers' Hall, and sat next my uncle, the Field-Marshal. He talked of his famous advance to Cabul through the Kyber Pass, relieving Jellalabad, and vindicating the honour and power of England after the previous disasters, and said, "I disobeyed orders, and might have been tried by a court martial and shot for it if I had not succeeded." This was the last time I saw him.

*27th February.*—To the Athenæum to see the procession pass of the Queen and Prince of Wales to St. Paul's, to return thanks for the Prince's recovery from his perilous attack of typhoid fever. On such an occasion it is interesting to watch the filling of the open space of Waterloo Place by the crowd. It is like seeing a carpet laid down to cover a bare floor. There was afterwards a great scramble for food in the dining-room of the club.

*9th March.*— Breakfast at Grant Duff's. Talk of Disraeli, his isolation in England, and his regarding his life among us rather as a drama than a reality. Once in the House of Commons he spoke of Her Majesty's company instead of H.M. Government. Dufferin said that in early life Disraeli was intimate with his mother and her sisters, the Duchess of Somerset and Mrs. Norton. At a grand reception given by Disraeli at the Foreign Office, at which the Prince and Princess of Wales were present, after doing the honours to them he came up to the Duchess of Somerset, and, pointing with his thumb over his shoulder in the direction of the

Royalties, said to her, "It's as good as a play—isn't it?"

11*th March.*—Dined with Sidney Colvin at Savile Club. Browning, F. T. Palgrave, Stopford Brooke, George Howard.

13*th March.*—Mr. Vanderweyer told me an anecdote of Talleyrand *apropos* to the misunderstanding about the Washington Treaty. At a diplomatic conference he pointed to a sentence, and remarked, "I suppose this means so and so." To which it was replied, "Cela va sans dire ;" and Talleyrand rejoined, "Oui, certainement, mais cela va mieux en le disant."

5*th April.*—To Leighton's studio to see the portrait painted by him of Sir Edward Ryan for the Dilettanti Society.

11*th April.*—To Lyceum. Irving in *Bells* and as Jeremy Diddler. He came into our box, and we then made for the first time the personal acquaintance of a man whose character and good qualities endear him to all who have the advantage of knowing him—generous almost to a fault, considerate, and always studying the good of those with whom he has to do.

18*th April.*—Houghton, who is a believer in the claimant in the Tichborne case, paid me a sovereign, to be returned if he is not convicted on the criminal charge of perjury.

*4th May.*—Visit to Grant Duffs at Hampden, rented by him. The house has some interesting points about it, but there are no relics of its great owner.

*8th May.*—Literary Fund Dinner, with the King of the Belgians in the chair.

*18th May.*—Visit to Edward Fitzgerald at Woodbridge. He has built himself a house—the Little Grange—in the outskirts of the town, but continues to live in his lodgings over a gunsmith's shop in the market-place. He put me up at his own charge at the principal inn. No man who has deserved so much fame for his writings was probably ever so modest and retiring. Our talk was chiefly of old days and old friends—J. M. Kemble, Thackeray, Spedding, Thompson, and others. In the neighbourhood he is regarded as a benevolent oddity.

*27th May.*—Breakfast at Lord Acton's, 58 Lowndes Square. There was a story of an Irish gentleman attending a levee at Dublin Castle, when Lord Spencer first appeared there as Viceroy, and was asked how he liked him, and said, "He's a deal too familiar; the man never saw me before and knew nothing about me, but he shook hands with me. I think much more of Lord Abercorn. He only looked at me over his beard, and treated me like the dirt under his feet." Lyceum in evening—Miss Bateman in *Leah*. Tyndall with us.

*8th June.*—Breakfast Club at Erskine May's. Bruce, H. Cowper, Grant Duff, Froude, Sir J. Lacaita, Sir John Lefevre, Sir W. S. Maxwell, Arthur Russell. Lord Dufferin was elected an honorary member on being appointed Governor-General of Canada, and during his administration of that office will not be expected to give or attend breakfasts.

*8th July.*—Lyceum. First night of *Medea*, in which Miss Bateman was very fine.

*9th July.*—First sitting to Ouless for my portrait at his studio in Bloomsbury Square. At the preceding private view of the Royal Academy exhibition I was much impressed by the excellence of a head in one of the rooms, and found another portrait by the same hand not far from it. Presently I fell in with Boxall, and asked him if he knew anything of Mr. Ouless, the painter of these two pictures.

He said he knew him well, and that he was a pupil of the Royal Academy of great promise. I asked, "Would he paint me?" and Boxall promised to give me an introduction to him for that purpose. A few days after I went accordingly to see Ouless, but when I mentioned my wish he said he was not a portrait painter; of the two pictures I had seen one was of his own father, and the other of an intimate friend—both done to please himself. He wanted to paint "history," and referred me to a picture by himself—a scene from the French Revolution, introducing Robespierre, which had been exhibited the previous year, of which he showed me a photograph. He was sorry to disappoint any friend of Boxall's, but he could not oblige me. We continued in conversation for some time, and at last he said he would make an exception in my case, and pleased me very much by promising to paint my portrait. He could not fix any price, as he had never before accepted a commission for a portrait, and this point was left to be decided by Boxall. I gave Ouless nineteen sittings, and the picture was well placed in the next exhibition of the Royal Academy. As a piece of fine colour I doubt whether he has since surpassed it, and, as far as I know, Ouless has never since painted anything but the excellent portraits which led to his early election as A.R.A. and R.A.

*13th July.*—Came to breakfast Browning, George Cayley, Holtzmann, etc. Browning told us that he had recently been presented with a contemporary portrait sketch of Count Guido Franceschini, evidently taken from him as he appeared on the scaffold for execution, with the name and date—*Conte Guido, etc., decapitato, etc.* It had been bought at a sale in London, and the purchaser thought that it should belong to the author of *The Ring and the Book.* He also told of Sheridan Knowles a story often told of Count D'Orsay. S. K. was complaining that he wanted to read a certain book and could not get it. A friend informed him of the existence of such things as circulating libraries, and S. K. took out and paid for a three months' subscription to Saunders & Ottley. He went into the country and stayed away more than three months, without getting out a book from their library. Then he went for a book, and was indignant at its being refused, on the ground that his subscription had expired. He said he had paid his guinea and had got nothing in return for it, and was furious. He was referred by the clerk at the counter to one of the principals, who explained the matter to him, but without appeasing his wrath. S. K. said, "It's a confounded swindle." The partner asked, "Do you mean to be personal, sir?" S. K., "No; on the contrary, if you are Saunders, d—n Ottley, and if you're Ottley, d—n Saunders."

*20th July.*—Dinner at home, to meet Madame de Mussy, her son and daughter, on a visit to London. Boxall, Kinglake, Browning, Hallé, and Miss Hallé.

*22d August.*—To Brussels, *viâ* Ostend. Bonn for a couple of nights. Heidelberg, three weeks. Nuremburg, Prague, Dresden for a fortnight. Home 1st October, by Hanover, Cologne, and Ostend.

*13th November.*—Dined alone with Sir William Boxall. He told me that his father was an Excise collector at Oxford with a salary of £200 a year, out of which he allowed him £50 a year to come to London and study art in or about the year 1817. He paid 8s. a week for lodgings in the neighbourhood of Brunswick Square, and used to dine at an eating-house for 8d. or 9d. His sister was married to Mr. Hickman, a silversmith and jeweller at Oxford, whose shop was visited for orders by a traveller from a firm in Clerkenwell. This man's name was Edwards, and he had at one time been a pupil of Banks the sculptor, but had abandoned the study of art and taken to trade at the time of the French Revolution in 1789, under the belief that such changes were about to take place in society as would destroy all demand for works of art. Edwards on one occasion saw a landscape drawing by Boxall, was struck by its merits, and asked to see the young artist. Boxall was at this time seventeen years old, and had not liked any of his father's plans for his future life. The introduction to Edwards led to his becoming a pupil at the Royal Academy, and determined his career.

# CHAPTER VIII

### THEATRE FRANCAIS

*5th March.*—To Paris for a week. During this visit on one afternoon I went over the Theatre Français under the guidance of Delaunay. The interior is more like that of a comfortable private house than that of a London theatre. The stairs from the artists' entrance are carpeted, and the walls of the staircase are hung with pictures. The *foyer des artistes* is a large well-furnished room, also hung with portraits of dramatic authors and actors. The *loges* or dressing-rooms of the *Sociétaires* are well-appointed and comfortable rooms. On the stage there is a sort of movable alcove for the performers to sit in who are engaged in the piece, so as to be sheltered from any draught of wind and close to their work. Any inconvenience, however, from the admission of too much air is not likely to occur at the Français. Close to the stage also there is a small subsidiary green-room for the convenience of the performers in making any adjustment in their costumes. The footlights are of oil and not of gas, which gives a peculiar softness to their light, and there is less heat, so that the sort of curtain of hot air which always dances over the footlights interferes less with perfect vision. On the stage the old grooves for the scenery have not been removed, but are not much in use. They mark the various *plans* of the stage, and here Delaunay, with only the *pompier* on duty and myself for audience, showed the difference of voice necessary to give effect to a stage whisper at each *plan*. Near to the audience the stage whisper was not much louder, although more distinct, than an ordinary whisper in private life. Retreating towards the back of the stage it became louder and louder, so that at the very farthest point from the footlights it was difficult to believe, when standing close to the actor, that it would be heard only as a whisper in the house. The next evening we attended the performance of *Marion de l'Orme*, with Delaunay as the Marquis de Saverny, the "*tout jeune homme blond, sans moustaches*" of Victor Hugo's stage direction, which Delaunay continued to be, with his inexhaustible youth and vivacity for so many years after this date. Mounet Sully, who transposed his names from Sully Mounet when he became an actor, was an admirable Didier. He was then commencing his eminent career, and gave way, perhaps, too much to some exaggerations, but showed all the promise of future success which has since been so amply fulfilled. Maubant was grand in the part of the Marquis de Nangis, the old feudal nobleman who brings his bodyguard of retainers with him to Paris from the country. Favart was the Marion de l'Orme in this magnificent representation of the most remarkable of Victor Hugo's historical dramas, in all ways equal to the best traditions of the place. Delaunay had kindly arranged that all the performers should be in the *foyer* during the longest *entr'acte*, and that we should see them assembled. It was very fine to see all the characters together, and as much at home in their rich costumes as if they were their usual clothes. Bressant, as Louis XIII., stood at the fireplace in his black suit, and looked so dignified that I almost knelt on one knee to do homage to him.

Mr. J. R. Lowell and his wife were at this time living in Paris at the Hotel Lorraine, in a street running parallel to the Rue du Bac, and we were fortunate enough to see something of them during our stay. The hotel was frequented by members of the Legitimist party, and by generally dining at the *table d'hôte* Lowell knew more about them than most people, and from him I learned a good deal which I could not otherwise have known. On one evening we dined with M. and Madame Mohl, and there met Renan and his wife, Brachet, and other people of interest. When Renan and Mohl were together they encouraged each other in the brilliant conversation in which both excelled. Renan's style in writing is beautiful, but yet not equal to his talk. The impression made by the two men was one not to be forgotten, and this meeting led to friendships of much subsequent profit and advantage. Renan had the most wit, and his conversation abounded with passages of luminous description, to which the strong and sound sense of Mohl sometimes afforded an interesting contrast. They were fast and intimate friends, and no difference of opinion ever interfered to alter the nature of their intercourse. On our last night I dined with Dr. De Mussy, while my wife and M—— went to see *Brittanicus* at the Français, taking with them Madame Mohl, who was delighted in an opportunity of going, for her husband hated the theatres, and never went near them. I joined them for the *Femmes Savantes*.

*24th April.*—At dinner R. W. Emerson and his daughter, Tyndall, Boxall, Clifford; and afterwards Henry Cowper and Laurence Oliphant. On the following Saturday Emerson came to the Breakfast Club at the house of Bruce.

*3d May.*—Macready's funeral at Kensall Green, from the Great Western Hotel, to which his remains had been removed from Cheltenham. The interment took place in his family vault beneath the chapel, and as the coffin sank slowly through an opening in the floor one could not avoid being reminded of the appliances of the theatrical stage—that stage for which he had done so much, and which had also done so much for him. Canon Fleming, one of his executors with myself, read the service with touching emotion, and spoke a few appropriate words before we separated at its close. There was a large and sympathetic attendance, representing the literature and dramatic art of two or three generations, and no man, by his private character and public services, better deserved such a testimony to his worth.

*12th May.*—To Princess's Theatre to see that charming actress Desclée in *Frou-frou*—a part in which she has never been approached by others who have attempted it. The natural gaiety and heedless selfishness of the early part of the character, driven into criminal indulgence by unworthy suspicions and jealousies, was given with consummate art. The grief and remorse of the end were tragic indeed. We afterwards saw her in *Diane de Lys,* which did not afford so much opportunity for the display of her powers.

*9th June.*—At dinner Joaquin Miller, Holtzmann, J. W. Clark, young Herman Merivale.

*18th June.*—C. C. S. dinner at Richmond—Fitzjames Stephen presided.

*28th June.*—Luncheon at home. Lady Castletown, Madame Mohl, Clemens (Mark

Twain) and his wife, Joaquin Miller, G. S. Venables, George Cayley.

*3d July.*—Mrs. Macready came to dine, and brought two manuscript volumes in quarto, containing Macready's autobiography and one of the diaries kept by him.

*4th July.*—Dined Houghton's, in Berkeley Square. Motley, Lord Rosebery, Lord Crewe, Mrs. Procter, etc. Being the anniversary of American Independence, Houghton made some remarks upon the occasion to Motley, who, looking at Rosebery, who sat opposite to him at table and looked much younger than his real age, said, " Perhaps our young friend does not understand what we are talking about ; " and got for reply, " Oh ! don't I. It's all about the bird of freedom, and that sort of bunkum." Afterwards to Lady Augusta Stanley, and had a beautiful moonlight view of the Abbey from the roof of the cloisters.

*2d August.*—To Tennyson at Aldworth for a couple of nights. He read " Vivien."

In this autumn some time was spent at Fontainebleau, where we enjoyed the beautiful and varied scenery of the forest, and the gardens and interior of the Chateau. Some of the finest bits of sylvan landscape to be seen anywhere exist round Fontainebleau. The trees are magnificent, especially the beeches. There are patches of heath, with birch trees and pools of water, which remind one of similar spots in the Highlands of Scotland. In other places there are masses of rock, covered with lichens of the richest colours, far surpassing in size and beauty those of similar formation to be seen at Eridge and Tunbridge Wells. Sometimes there is a view of distant country, and at other times one feels lost in the depths of a thick forest. The provisions made to prevent strangers from losing their way are very complete. There are sign-posts and arrow-marks and "blazings" on the bark of conspicuous trees, all arranged on a regular system, so that one may stray farther than was intended, but, by daylight at least, cannot fail to find the way back to the town.

One day we drove to Barbison, the artist's village on the outskirts of the forest, where Jean François Millet lived and painted. We had been told that he received visitors without any introduction, and we rang at the door of his house, one side of which was in the village street, while a low-walled garden separated the door of the studio from the roadway. The door was opened to us by his wife, who said that her husband would be able to see us at the end of an hour. We strolled about, and returned to find the great painter in *blouse* and *sabots* in his painting-room, which more resembled the rough workshop of a village carpenter than the studio of an artist. Millet's manner was frank and courteous, and he put aside his work to receive us. His figure was erect and squarely built, and he had a handsome face with large gray eyes, a wide brow, a bright complexion, and a true and winning smile. He showed us all he had to show. There was a magnificent unfinished picture, which he called "Le Coup de Vent." It represented a huge oak uprooted by a hurricane and in the act of falling, with a man escaping from it; a dark stormy sky, full of the tragic passion of a beautiful country suddenly struck by ruin and despair. The question was asked, "Est-ce dans la forêt?" Millet replied, "Madame, c'est partout." The other subject in progress was that of a flock of sheep feeding. Millet spoke of the quiet and serene happiness which he wished here to represent, but further conversation with him was stopped by the arrival of another person, who looked like a Jew picture-dealer, and talked much nonsense about art. He remarked, "Enfin, Monsieur, j'ai la maladie des Millets;" to which the painter replied, "Mais, Monsieur, prenez donc de la medicine;" and we thought it best to come away and leave the gentleman to take his physic if he chose. By getting one day into conversation with a certain M. Trapoz, who had permission to paint in the Chateau, and had a pass-key to all the rooms, we saw some of the apartments, which are not usually shown. In this way we were admitted to the rooms of Madame de Maintenon, those occupied by Pope Pius VII. when a state prisoner of the first Napoleon's, and the *Galeries de Henri II.* and *des Cerfs*, in the latter of which the unfortunate Monaldeschi was executed by order of Christina, Queen of Sweden, and where the secret coat of chain-mail worn by him is to be seen.

Afterwards in Paris we enjoyed a good deal of play-going. At the Français we saw Mounet Sully and Sara Bernhardt in *Phèdre;* and Thiron, Croizette, and Thomassin in the pretty little piece *L'été de St. Martin;* and Delaunay in *L'Ecole des Femmes*. We heard and saw the *Hamlet* of Ambroise Thomas at the Grand Opera, then in its old quarters, Rue Lepeletier, with Faure, whom I always count among the good representatives of Hamlet. Two evenings were pleasantly spent in Delaunay's apartment at the top of the house, Rue Luxemburg (since changed to Rue Cambon), listening to readings by him from Alfred de Musset, one of which was of the *Nuit d'Octobre*. After this we saw him in his great part in *Le Menteur*, and on the same night had Got and Favart in the *Supplice d'une Femme;* and I was introduced to Regnier in the *foyer*. At the Gaieté there was an amusing melodrame called *Le Gascon*, in which La Fontaine and his wife acted. There was a third and a fourth evening at Delaunay's, when he gave us one of his most effective readings. He read *La grande mère* of Beranger; and also *La Cigue* and other things of Beranger's. Our last evening in Paris was spent at the Français to see Marivaux's charming old piece of *L'amour à hasard*. During this visit we had the pleasure of seeing a good deal of Madame Mohl, and also of Lord and Lady

Lytton, he then being the First Secretary in the British Embassy. One evening in the well-known rooms in the Rue du Bac, we were much interested by the recital of M. Mohl's experiences of Paris in the days of the Commune, during which, and the subsequent siege from Versailles, he was in Paris, and alone. He said that no houses were burnt in which any one remained to offer resistance. At the *Ministère de la Marine*, in the *Place de la Concorde*, every preparation had been made for its destruction by petroleum, and it only remained to apply the match. On the night of the intended burning the only person in the building was a gouty old *concièrge*, who would not desert his post. A *pétroleur* presented himself, and said he had orders to light the petroleum. The porter remonstrated, and asked the man if he wished to do so great a mischief. The man replied, No; but he must obey his orders and earn his day's pay. "How much do you get for doing it?"—"Ten francs a day."—"Then I will give you twenty francs not to do it."—"No; I am an honest man, and must do my duty." "Very well, then," said the porter, "you will burn the building, but you will also perish in it yourself; I am not going to stay to be burnt, and as I have the keys I shall lock the door as I go out, and you will remain to die by your own work." This moved the man, and he said, "Give me the twenty francs and I will go." And so the Admiralty of Paris was saved. Mohl said there was never any plunder; the inhabitants of the houses to be destroyed always had a few minutes' warning to leave and take with them whatever they could. The *Grand Livre* of the Public Debt was burnt in the *Ministère de Finance*, but a duplicate existed, and there was no inconvenience. The registers of births and marriages were all destroyed by fire at the *Hotel de Ville*, and a bureau was opened to which all persons were invited to come with the best materials they could supply for their reconstruction. It is supposed that many children born out of wedlock, whose legitimation was desired, were put on the register as legitimate in this way. Some marriages, on the other hand, may have been purposely left without legal registration.

11*th October.*—Lunched at Athenæum with Lacaita, Lord Justice James, Sir Francis

Grant, Richmond, Ward, Herbert, come from the funeral of Edwin Landseer in St. Paul's.

*15th October.*—Edward Herries came to dinner to say good-bye on returning to his diplomatic duties in Rome. When he was attached to the British Legation at Lisbon he saw at Cintra the house shown as that in which the famous Convention of Cintra was signed. The table on which it was signed is to be seen in the house, with the splashes of ink which fell from the pen of the Duke of Wellington, then Sir Arthur Wellesley. In point of fact, the Convention was not signed at Cintra, nor by the Duke of Wellington. It was signed by Sir Hew Dalrymple at Lisbon, and transmitted home by him in a letter dated "Cintra," where he was staying. Hence it came to be called the Convention of Cintra, and the local legend was invented, and the house and table provided to support it. In the same way it may be strongly doubted whether the table shown at Fontainebleau as that on which Napoleon the First signed his abdication is a genuine historical piece of furniture.

*10th November.*—At a special Managers'

Meeting at the Royal Institution an address of condolence was agreed to for the family of Sir Henry Holland, our late President, and I was requested to write it. We also unanimously agreed to propose the Duke of Northumberland as the new President.

*3d December.*—Dined with Froude in Onslow Gardens, and with him to Westminster Abbey to hear Max Müller lecture on Missions in the nave, and then to tea at the Deanery. It was considered a daring innovation of Stanley's to allow a layman to speak in the Abbey.

*31st January* 1874.—Dinner at the Albion, given by members of the Northern Circuit to Martin on his retirement from the bench. Eighty-five men were present. Pickering made an excellent chairman.

*12th April.*—Lunch with Sir Charles Lyell, who was good enough to be pleased with a review of mine in *Fraser* on his *Antiquity of Man.* To W. K. Clifford's lecture at St. George's Hall upon "Speculations on the Duration of the Universe." Dined with Irving at Garrick Club. Met Critchett, Bateman, Toole, Lewis Wingfield, Monckton, Edmund Yates,

Bancroft, Sir Baldwin Leighton, Hamilton Aidé, Levy (*Daily Telegraph*). Toole had a story of how he was once engaged to act for two nights at Portsmouth. He found the town placarded with bills, " Mr. Toole's first appearance in Portsmouth." The next day it was " Mr. Toole's farewell benefit." Bateman had one of an indolent actor who, being told at rehearsal to change his side of exit in one scene, was heard grumbling to himself, " What! more study."

*4th May.*—George Grove called by appointment from Macmillans to see Macready's reminiscences and his diaries, afterwards published by Macmillans for Mrs. Macready, under my editorship.

*10th May.*—To Paris. The next day took to the Theatre Français my wife's present of books for their library—Booth's reprint of the first folio of Shakespeare, and the poetical works of Byron and Henry Taylor. At night there was the *Il ne faut jurer de rien*, with the splendid cast of Got, Delaunay, Talbot, Plessy, Reichemberg; and the next night the *Sphinx*, in which Croizette's acting was making much sensation; and the following night *La belle*

*Poule*, a first representation, with Sara Bernhardt.

14*th May.*—Dined with Delaunay. He and Mdlle. Reichemberg recited a scene from *L'Ecole des Maris*, and also from La Fontaine and Beranger.

15*th May.*—Dined Mohls. Met Renan, Leon Say, Delaroches.

16*th May.*—Called on Victor Hugo, 21 Rue de Clichy, upon a letter of introduction from Sidney Colvin. The poet was on the verge of a *déménagement*, and could not receive us in his accustomed way. But it was no matter to us that his reception rooms were dismantled; indeed it was all the better for us, as we had him to ourselves, only Madame —— being present besides. He was at this time a man of a kingly presence, very erect, dignified in movement, and if his face was not positively handsome, it was very powerful—his wide brow, flashing eyes, and firm-set mouth announced genius and determination; and his voice was resonant and capable of the most varied expression. He was very courteous, taking care to include each of us—we were three—in his conversation. After some general talk he asked my wife, who was seated beside him, whether she cared for plays, and she spoke to him of the Théâtre Français, and of the performance of *Marion de l'Orme*. This led him on to some inquiries as to existing English actors, and he spoke of Macready, whom he had seen in Paris, with admiration. He then spoke of Garrick, and asked my wife whether she had read much about him, and seen all the portraits of him. She said, Yes, the records of him interested her, but she had a quarrel with him, as he had chosen, for purposes of his own, to create a new Shakespeare, and almost obliterate the original text, and lead the public to worship a false god. Victor Hugo was excited by these observations, followed them with enthusiasm, and now and then substituted some more forcible word for the one used by my wife; and finally, taking her hand in his, he said, " C'est absolument vrai. Madame, vous êtes une femme charmante." The conversation was carried on in French, for the poet could not speak English; it was long and varied in subject, and on his part eloquent and striking—hardly less so than are his writings.

*19th June.*—Wendell Holmes (son of Oliver,

and the colonel who was reported as killed in
the American Civil War; now a judge in his
own country, and an accomplished jurist)
came to sit by my side in Judges' Chambers
to see our practice. Afterwards I took him
to see the Inner Temple Library, the Middle
Temple Hall, and the Public Record Office.
He was much moved by the sight of Domesday Book. The Americans seem to feel more
reverence for our antiquities than we do ourselves, and indeed Domesday is an unique
historical record. Wendell Holmes came with
his agreeable wife to breakfast with us a few
days afterwards.

18*th December.*—I was appointed Queen's
Remembrancer by Mr. Disraeli, in succession
to my good friend and colleague, Sir William
Henry Walton, who had held the post for seventeen years, and retired from that and his Master's
place in the Court of Exchequer, in which his service had been much longer, carrying with him the
regrets and good wishes of all who knew him, and
receiving the well-earned honour of knighthood.
As one of the Commissioners whose labours
and recommendations led to the framing and
passing of the Common Law Procedure Acts of

1852 and 1854, and one or two which followed them, he did admirable service in giving most important aid towards perfecting measures of legal reform, in the subsequent working of which there was nothing but success to be recorded. This happy result was largely due to the composition of the Commission, which embraced judges, counsel, solicitors, and, in the person of Walton, a most able and experienced representative of the official experience, naturally most conversant with the daily routine and practice of Common Law business. It was thought proper to pursue a different course in the preparation of the more recent Judicature Acts. From the beginning the Common Law Procedure Acts worked smoothly, with no increase of costs to the suitors, with no excessive multiplication of appeals, with no derangement of the circuits, or interference with the due despatch of business in London; and their success was firmly established in fewer months than the years during which the Judicature Acts have been in operation. With all the merit which must be conceded to the latest efforts of legal reform, in having remedied the strange anomaly of having two sets of tribunals not guided by the same rules of law, and of opening the way to future simplifications and further reductions of establishments and public expenditure, it cannot be denied that they have created many fresh evils in the process of endeavouring to find a complete remedy for old ones.

The recent history of the ancient office of Queen's Remembrancer, which dates at least from the reign of Henry II., is a curious one. Up to the year 1823 it was held by the Right Hon. Thomas Steele, who had been one of Pitt's right-hand men, and was long one of the secretaries of the Treasury. It was not a sinecure, but the actual duties were performed by deputy, and it may be presumed that the bulk of the fees received went to the titular holder of the office. Upon the death of Steele in 1823 the office was conferred upon Mr. Henry Vincent, then private secretary to Mr. Herries at the Treasury, in the view, as was understood, of its immediate modification, but he continued to hold it with a fixed salary until 1857. It was then provided by a special Act regulating the office that it should henceforth be held, to borrow an ecclesiastical phrase, *in commendam* with a Mastership in the Exchequer; the Master to be selected by the Treasury, and to be remunerated by an additional amount of salary. On the passing of the Judicature Acts, when the three old Common Law Courts were merged in one as the Queen's Bench, it was provided that the office of Queen's Remembrancer should be held by the Senior Master for the time being, and so the matter now stands.

I have so often been asked to tell what are the duties of the Queen's Remembrancer by ladies and others who do not study bluebooks and Acts of Parliament, that I may as well now try to describe them. The Queen's Remembrancer is at the head of the department which has charge of all Revenue suits, formerly belonging to the old Court of Exchequer, and now transferred to the Queen's Bench. These would comprise all proceedings by the Crown for the recovery of income and assessed taxes, succession, legacy, and probate duties, or for the recovery of land or rents due to the Crown. The preparation of the lists of sheriffs for the counties of England and Wales, for use in Court on the Morrow of St. Martin, and of the parchment rolls to be pricked by the Queen, and other matters pertaining to the execution of the office of sheriff, also belong to the department of the Queen's Remembrancer. It is the duty, too, of that officer, as has been already incidentally mentioned, to attend at the nomination of sheriffs on the Morrow of St. Martin. There are also some interesting duties to be performed, but of a far less onerous and responsible nature. He has to attend as the officer of the Queen's Bench when the Lord Mayor makes his appearance on the 9th of November every year to take the declaration of office, in recent times substituted for the ancient oath. He also represents the old Court of Exchequer upon the occasion of the city of London doing suit and service, in discharge of quit rents, for certain land and tenements anciently held under the Crown— a ceremony which was formerly performed in open court before all the Barons, and in more recent times before an abolished official called the Cursitor Baron, but which now takes place in the Queen's Remembrancer's room. The City Solicitor produces horse-shoes and nails, which he counts in respect of a forge which formerly existed near St. Clement Danes in the Strand; and chops representative faggots with an axe and a bill-hook, in respect of certain land in Shropshire. Probably the ancient tenures were by the actual services of shoeing one or more of the king's horses annually, and of providing a certain quantity of firewood for the king. It is a very curious and interesting survival, and is almost the only one of the actual rendering of old feudal services. The flags annually sent to the Queen from Blenheim and Strathfieldsay are, of course, of the creation of modern times, and belong to the species of tenure formerly known as "Grand Serjeantry." I trust that I was considered by the authorities of the city of London to have properly discharged the duties which brought me into connection with them, and I shall always feel deeply grateful for the hospitable return made to me by the constant invitations with which I was favoured during my time of office—to the Guildhall banquet on Lord Mayor's day, to the dinner given to the Judges at the Mansion House, and to other municipal festivities. The dinner on the 9th November in the Guildhall is one of the finest and grandest entertainments that can be imagined, with its hundreds of guests in full dress entertained in that magnificent hall, and the unique interest it has enjoyed for so many years in the presence of the Ministers for the time being, and the expectation that some indications of political intentions will be afforded on the occasion. The speeches which it was my good fortune to hear made on these occasions by Disraeli were admirable specimens of after-dinner speaking, and were delivered with an air of high comedy about them which made them delightful to listen to. But in the Guildhall, as in so many smaller places where there is less excuse for it, one had with most of the speakers to complain of their not being audible. Now, I venture to hold that every man who has to speak in public, whether after dinner or on other occasions, ought to take some amount of pains, by previous exercise and instruction, to secure the comfort of his audience by being easily heard, and to save himself from the interruptions and hints to stop which I have so often seen ludicrously mistaken for applause. This is within the reach of every one with the natural gifts of speech, and who is free from vocal weakness and defects, and it ought to be done, or at least attempted.

Another very pleasant function incident to the office of Queen's Remembrancer was that of presiding at the annual Trial of the Pyx, held at Goldsmiths' Hall. In former times the trials of the purity of the coinage were held at uncertain intervals, and at distances of several years. All the specimen coins put into the Pyx or box appropriated for the purpose were then produced at Westminster, from the Treasure-house in the Abbey, where the Pyx was kept, and a jury of goldsmiths being sworn, they assayed and weighed the gold and silver coins, frequently under the presidence of the Sovereign in person. Once Prince Rupert presided, and from his fondness for scientific pursuits he must have taken great interest in the proceedings. During the last century, and for the first half of the present one, the jury were sworn before the Lord Chancellor for the time being, or sometimes before an Archbishop. Upon one occasion Mr. Pitt presided as Chancellor of the Exchequer. Under the provisions of the existing Coinage Act the trial of the Pyx now occurs annually at Goldsmiths' Hall, which offers all necessary conveniences for the processes of assaying and weighing the coins. The appointment of the presiding officer rests with the Treasury, and under the present system the Queen's Remembrancer has always been the officer so appointed. The precision to which the purity of the gold and silver coinage, in accordance with the prescribed standards, has been brought is a marvel of accuracy; and during all the time that I had to sign and return the verdict of the Pyx jury to the Treasury, it went on improving until there was no further room for improvement. The day's proceedings always closed with a very pleasant function of civic hospitality in the form of a dinner in Goldsmiths' Hall, where those who had been at work during the morning had their labours recognised by special toasts in their honour, to which the chief officials of the Mint were invited, and which was often graced by the presence of the Chancellor of the Exchequer or other Ministers. In two or three years one got to know all the usual guests and many of the entertainers, and it became to me one of the most truly festive and agreeable dinners of the season. The year after I quitted office the Goldsmiths' Company were so good as again to ask me to this dinner, and I accepted their invitation with great pleasure, to meet all my old friends once more in the character of Dowager Queen's Remembrancer.

THE END

*Printed by* R. & R. Clark, *Edinburgh.*

www.ingramcontent.com/pod-product-compliance
Lightning Source LLC
Chambersburg PA
CBHW032123230426
43672CB00009B/1838